Inside the CIA

Inside the CIA

The Architecture, Art & Atmosphere of America's Premier Intelligence Agency

By F. Clifton Berry Jr.

Inside the CIA: The Architecture, Art & Atmosphere of America's Premier Intelligence Agency

By F. Clifton Berry Jr.

Community Communications, Inc.
Publishers: Ronald P. Beers and James E. Turner

Staff for *Inside the CIA*
Executive Editor: James E. Turner
Managing Editor: Linda Moeller Pegram
Design Director: Camille Leonard
Designer: Chris Elliott
Photo Editors: F. Clifton Berry Jr., Chris Elliott and Linda M. Pegram
Production Manager: Cindy Lovett
Editorial Assistants: Katrina Williams and Kari Collin
Proofreader: Wynona B. Hall
Research Associates: Sheree L. Storm and Jeffrey B. St. Onge
Accounting Services: Sara Ann Turner
Printing Production: Frank Rosenberg/GSAmerica

COMMUNITY
COMMUNICATIONS

Montgomery, Alabama

James E. Turner, Chairman of the Board
Ronald P. Beers, President
Daniel S. Chambliss, Vice President

Every effort has been made to ensure the accuracy of the information herein. However, Community Communications is not responsible for any errors or omissions which might have occurred.

Dedication

This book is created as a tribute to the men and women of the Central Intelligence Agency past and present. They work in the shadows so the rest of us may enjoy the sunshine.

Table of Contents

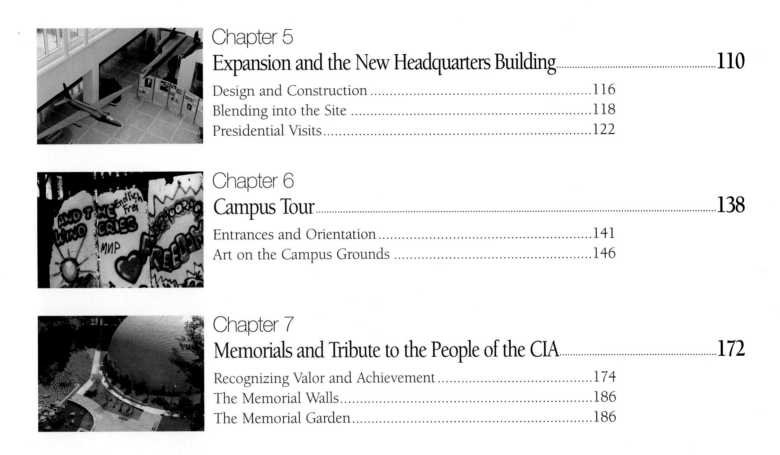

Acknowledgments

Creation of this peek inside the Central Intelligence Agency's headquarters buildings and campus
has been made possible by the cooperation of dozens of persons inside the CIA and
elsewhere. Most of them must necessarily remain anonymous.

However, it is possible to mention the names of three whose contributions have been essential.
Carlos D. Davis, Chairman of the CIA Fine Arts Commission, inspired creation of the book
and brought his encyclopedic knowledge of the environment, the buildings, and their
contents to the project and enriched it immeasurably. Herbert E. Hetu, Director of
the CIA50 Program Office, skillfully coordinated the development of the project
and fit it into the overall program of observances of the CIA's 50th anniversary.
His inspiration continued throughout the preparation to fruition. His associate,
Denise Standley, contributed creative ideas and performed countless
reality checks and wonders of coordination.

Special tribute and thanks go to the Photography Branch of the Printing and Photography Group
of the CIA. Their names cannot be cited, but we all can acknowledge their terrific
command of their professional craft. Their talents, experience, and cooperation
truly made the visual impact of this book possible.

The author is grateful to Weidenfeld & Nicholson, publishers, for permission to quote from
For Lust of Knowing; Memoirs of an Intelligence Officer, by Archie Roosevelt (1988).

Foreword

Within the pages of this book are photos and text that take the reader on an "insider's tour" of the campus of the Central Intelligence Agency and into its two headquarters buildings. All of the text and all of the photos are unclassified. The reader will not find cloaks or daggers here, but will discover a rich trove of photos that have not been seen outside the CIA (and many which will be seen inside the organization for the first time in these pages).

Most of the documents and photos were provided by various offices of the CIA, with appropriate care. The CIA's Fine Arts Commission, in furtherance of its mission to ensure compliance with esthetic standards in nature, and with its guiding principles, was an especially fruitful source of materials and of guidance.

My intention is to provide the reader with the sense of the campus-like environment where the men and women of the CIA headquarters work. In the process we will share the privilege of going through the visitor control points and stroll the corridors in a tour that is otherwise impossible.

The information and photos came from multiple sources. We made every effort to ensure accuracy. Any errors that may have crept in are inadvertent.
—F. Clifton Berry Jr.
Northern Virginia, 1997

At the author's request, the CIA's Publications Review Board has reviewed the manuscript of this book to assist the author in eliminating classified information. The CIA poses no security objection to its publication. This review should not be construed as an official release of information, confirmation of its accuracy, or an endorsement of the author's views.

Chapter One

Early Years: The E Street Complex

The Central Intelligence Agency (CIA) came into existence on September 18, 1947. It was created as one of the provisions of the National Security Act of 1947. President Harry S. Truman signed the bill into law on July 26 of that year. The bill established the Office of the Secretary of Defense, the National Security Council, the United States Air Force as a separate military branch, and the CIA. Section 102(a) of the Act spelled it out: "There is established under the National Security Council, a Central Intelligence Agency with a Director of Central Intelligence who shall be the head thereof."

Previous page, left **Section 2 of the Central Intelligence Act of 1949 provided for a seal of office for the CIA. President Truman's Executive Order 10111 of February 17, 1950, approved and set forth the design. The American Eagle is the national bird and is a symbol of strength and alertness. The radiating spokes of the compass rose depict the coverage of intelligence data from all areas of the world to a central point.**

Previous page, right **Northwest Washington, DC, during World War II. View is westward. In the foreground on the right is the Apex Building, aptly describing its position at the apex of the Federal Triangle. The building sits between Sixth and Seventh Streets at the intersection of Pennsylvania Avenue on the right and Constitution Avenue proceeding straight west to the Potomac River. Maj. Gen. William J. Donovan and staff occupied offices in the Apex Building early in the war, while he was Coordinator of Information. They moved from there to the 2430 E Street Complex as the staff grew and the organization became the Office of Strategic Services. Temporary wartime office buildings are seen on the Capitol Mall past the Washington Monument. Photo: The National Archives.**

Opposite page **Sign on the chain-link fence proclaims the entrance to the E Street Complex of the Central Intelligence Agency in downtown Washington. This sign, "2430 E St. NW," dates back to the CIA's founding. It is on display in the Library at the Langley headquarters.**

Left **Central Building was completed in 1904. It served as a Marine hospital until World War II. When William J. Donovan took over the E Street facility during WW II, it housed the Deputy Director for Intelligence and other activities. Later it reverted to the Agency's medical facility.**

Opposite page **Building 7 was one of the numbered buildings in the E Street Complex. Building numbers ranged as high as 14. Other buildings had compass point names such as East or South, while letters such as I, J, K, L, M, and Q were assigned to additional buildings.**

According to the law, the Central Intelligence Agency and the United States Air Force would be activated on the day after the new Secretary of Defense took the oath of office. James V. Forrestal was sworn in as Secretary of Defense on September 17, and the CIA and Air Force were activated the next day.

Heritage

The new CIA had an illustrious heritage from its wartime predecessor, the Office of Strategic Services (OSS). The need for accurate and timely intelligence, which had proved instrumental in achieving victory in World War II, dated back to the Revolutionary War.

Gen. George Washington appreciated the value of intelligence, the gathering of timely information about enemy intentions and capabilities. In the fight for independence, he created an intelligence apparatus and made use of its products in his campaign decisions.

The Battle of Trenton provides an example of Washington's use of timely intelligence in tactical planning. In the late autumn of 1776 the patriot cause looked bleak. Continental forces had suffered a series of battlefield defeats. Washington had been forced to retreat from New York across New Jersey, escaping across the Delaware River just ahead of the pursuing British. Although his army was safe for a time while the British settled into winter quarters, this security was not destined to last much longer. Many of the troops succumbed to disease and others had deserted. Worse yet, the enlistments of the majority of the remaining army would expire on December 31.

Washington needed to achieve a victory at this crucial moment. Timely intelligence enabled him to do so. A patriot butcher impersonating a Tory acquired knowledge of the size of the Hessian garrison in Trenton, New Jersey, just across the Delaware River. It constituted 1,400 men. The butcher-spy also learned that the Hessian commander, Colonel Rall, drank heavily and that camp security was lax.

That knowledge enabled Washington to formulate a plan to cross the Delaware River on Christmas night and surprise the Hessians with an assault in the early morning of December 26. The plan worked and resulted in a decisive and opportune victory that invigorated his army and furthered the patriot cause. Washington then scored another victory at Princeton, driving the British out of New Jersey. Recruiting surged along with the new spirit of confidence stimulated by the twin victories.

A few months after the battles at Trenton and Princeton, Washington wrote to Col. Elias Dayton on July 26, 1777:

"The necessity of procuring good intelligence is apparent & need not be further urged—all that remains for me to add, is, that you keep the whole matter as secret as possible. For upon Secrecy, Success depends in most Enterprizes of the kind, and for want of it, they are generally defeated, however well planned and promising a favourable issue."

A copy of the letter is on display in the CIA Headquarters.

Subsequent presidents recognized the value of intelligence as George Washington had, usually more so in wartime than during the long periods of peace enjoyed

"The necessity of procuring good intelligence is apparent & need not be further urged—all that remains for me to add, is, that you keep the whole matter as secret as possible. For upon Secrecy, Success depends in most Enterprizes of the kind, and for want of it, they are generally defeated, however well planned and promising a favourable issue."

Gen. George Washington

Right **Even the birdhouses at the CIA compound were given building numbers. Here is Building 12-1/2.**

by the United States during its first 165 years.

By 1941 the war in Europe was widespread, and the United States' mobilization had begun. On July 11 of that year President Franklin D. Roosevelt appointed William J. Donovan to the post of Coordinator of Information. Donovan, a prominent New York lawyer, had earned the Medal of Honor in World War I combat for his service as a colonel. He set up the Coordinator of Information offices next to the White House in rooms 246, 247, and 248 of the building on Seventeenth Street that housed the War, State, and Navy Departments. It is now called the Old Executive Office Building. Before long the Coordinator of Information staff moved into space in the Apex Building. It forms the tip of the complex of office buildings called the "Federal Triangle" in downtown Washington.

The Japanese employed military intelligence and deception to attack Pearl Harbor on December 7, 1941. The morning raid by carrier-based airplanes devastated United States military power in the Pacific. The blow surprised and galvanized the population and leadership of the United States. On June 13, 1942, President Roosevelt established the Office of Strategic Services to replace the Office of Coordinator of Information. Donovan continued as director, remaining a civilian until being appointed brigadier general on March 24, 1943. He directed the OSS throughout World War II.

With its missions and staff expanding, General Donovan moved the OSS headquarters into buildings near the east bank of the Potomac River in the northwest quadrant of downtown Washington, DC. The site was on nineteen acres of land acquired in 1790 by George Washington's new federal government. This land had been owned by the Davidson and Burnes families before becoming government property known as Federal Reservation 4. (The White House was Federal Reservation 1.)

Although the government acquired the land in 1790, it

was not put to use for more than half a century. Finally, in 1844, the Washington Observatory was established on the site under control of the United States Navy. The Navy operated the observatory for fifty years. However, as nearby Tyber Creek silted up and evolved into an odorous marsh, the Navy moved the observatory to higher ground on Massachusetts Avenue in northwest Washington, DC. The creation and paving of Constitution Avenue obliterated the marsh, and the site became home to hospitals and medical research activities of the Navy and Public Health Service.

New buildings were constructed on the site to house those activities, beginning in 1903 and continuing into the early 1930s. This site became known in Washington as the E Street Complex. The cornerstone of the headquarters building, named the Administration Building, was laid in 1932. The Administration Building became General Donovan's wartime headquarters and was nicknamed "the Kremlin" by its denizens.

As the OSS missions expanded, so did its need for office space to house its headquarters and key activities. Additional permanent buildings at the E Street Complex became home to OSS activities. The buildings were designated by numbers such as 7, 8, 13, 14 and compass points such as East and South.

Existing office space in Washington, DC, could not adequately meet the wartime demands of all branches of the government, OSS included. President Roosevelt responded to the needs for office space by directing the

building of several temporary structures ("tempos") on vacant space in Washington, which included the Capitol Mall. The tempos were not built to endure; they were intended for destruction when the war was over.

The OSS moved its operations into several of those tempos near the Tidal Basin and Reflecting Pool on the Mall. The drab numbering system of the buildings seemed appropriate for the lackluster appearance of the structures. The tempos were given letter designations such as M and Q.

Let one of the CIA members who worked in the buildings in the late 1950s tell what the tempo buildings were like. Archie Roosevelt served in military intelligence during World War II and in the CIA later. In his memoir entitled *For Lust of Knowing,* he described working life in the tempos:

"They were dilapidated, impractical, hard to heat or cool, yet we developed a certain affection for them. We were all within reach of each other in well-defined territories along the corridor connecting all the buildings. We walked together at noon by the pool in warm weather, and those sufficiently high in the hierarchy to enjoy offices with windows facing the pool and the Lincoln Memorial could gaze out at the skaters in winter. Others in the back wings could at least contemplate their colleagues at work in the buildings next door, giving us a comfortable sense of camaraderie and intimacy.

"Sometimes this propinquity led to security problems, and windows had to be screened off to prevent other elements of the Agency from seeing papers or maps they had no need to know about. At least in one case I know of, it

Opposite page **South Building was the largest on the E Street Complex. It was built in the early 1930s and served as a naval hospital until World War II. The Research and Development Branch was among its occupants during the OSS days of World War II.**

led also to personal embarrassment. One of my friends, working in his second-floor office on a weekend, happened to look down and see a colleague in an office below in the process of undressing a pretty secretary, with the obvious intention of committing a bit of unauthorized covert action.

"Surrendering to an irresistible impulse, my friend picked up the phone, dialed his colleague, and watched him draw away from the lady to answer it.

" 'This is God speaking,' said a deep commanding voice. 'I see what you are doing. It is a grievous sin.' "

"He hung up and saw the parties separating...."

Central Intelligence Agency is Created

Soon after he was promoted to major general early in November 1944, General Donovan wrote a memorandum to President Roosevelt about planning for national intelligence capabilities in the coming postwar era. In the memo, General Donovan recommended the establishment of a central intelligence service, which would be a civilian agency to coordinate all the intelligence services, including correlating the intelligence material collected by all government agencies. This proposed agency would be authorized to conduct activities abroad, but would have "no police or law enforcement functions, either at home or abroad."

In the week before his death, President Roosevelt replied to Donovan:

"Apropos of your memorandum of November 18, 1944, relative to the establishment of a central intelligence service, I should appreciate your calling together the chiefs of the foreign intelligence and national security units in the various executive agencies, so that a consensus of opinion can be secured."

Franklin D. Roosevelt died one week later, but the concept of a central entity for intelligence matters persisted through the end of the war and into the immediate postwar period of demobilization. Victory came in Europe one month after FDR's death, and the Japanese surrendered in Tokyo Bay aboard the battleship USS *Missouri* on September 2, 1945.

Demobilization and a return to peace resulted in the dismantling of the mighty military machine and the intelligence apparatus that been instrumental in winning the war. President Harry S. Truman signed Executive Order 9621 on October 1, 1945. It abolished the Office of Strategic Services and transferred its functions to the State and War Departments. Three months later Truman established the Central Intelligence Group to coordinate existing departmental intelligence. He named Rear Adm. Sidney W. Souers, USNR, the current deputy chief of naval intelligence, to the position of Director of Central Intelligence (DCI). Admiral Souers was sworn in on January 23, 1946. Five months later, on June 10, 1946, Lt. Gen. Hoyt S. Vandenberg, USA, succeeded Admiral Souers. He served in the post almost a year, until May 1, 1947. Rear Adm. Roscoe H. Hillenkoetter, USN, was sworn in on that day and served for more than three years.

The euphoria of peace soon gave way to the tensions of the Cold War and turbulence in trouble spots around the world. The national requirements for intelligence collec-

Left "The Kremlin" was the nickname given to East Building by its occupants during World War II. Before the war it was headquarters of the medical and public health facilities at E Street. Gen. William J. Donovan set up his office in the southwest corner of the first floor. Allen Dulles began his tenure as Director of Central Intelligence in the same office, but moved over to South Building.

Right **Building M was a wartime "tempo" wooden building across the Capitol Mall from the E Street Complex and nearer the Potomac River.**

tion and analysis expanded. The E Street Complex remained the heart of the national intelligence effort.

President Truman was aware of the rivalries among the services and among the several organizations responsible for conducting intelligence activities. The War Department had its intelligence division, as did the Navy. The Departments of State, Treasury, Commerce, and Agriculture, and the Federal Bureau of Investigation had operations overseas.

President Truman knew that the scattered activities of the agencies and departments could not provide him or his successors the necessary facts for reliable decisions on foreign and military policy. He knew that reorganization was necessary, but not at the cost of worsening interdepartmental rivalries.

The National Security Act of 1947 provided the solution. The National Security Council and Central Intelligence Agency came into being, as did the separate Air Force. The assignments given to the CIA followed pretty closely to General Donovan's plan of November 1944 and President Truman's directive of January 1946, which included prohibitions on police power and internal security functions.

The CIA was created at an opportune time to play a central role in national security and foreign policy as the Cold War heated up. Civil war in Greece, the Berlin Blockade, and the Korean War were among the crises demanding coordinated intelligence. Admiral Hillenkoetter served as Director of Central Intelligence into the early months of the Korean War. Army Gen. Walter Bedell Smith

succeeded him in the DCI office at the E Street Complex on October 7, 1950, serving until February 1953.

Need to Relocate

Many activities of the CIA continued in the former OSS office space in the World War II temporary buildings, including some in West Potomac Park that had been wartime barracks for members of the Women's Army Corps. As more space was required in the postwar era, employees moved into commercial and government properties around the city.

Offices in the temporary buildings and other improvised quarters were crowded, noisy, and uncomfortable. They were also expensive to guard and to maintain. There were no secure phones, and all documents for coordination had to be hand-carried among the several locations.

Relief for the scattered overcrowding was desirable, but it did not begin for more than a decade after the CIA was founded.

President Truman's second term ended on January 20, 1953. Two months earlier, after Dwight D. Eisenhower was elected as his successor, Truman visited the CIA. During his visit on November 21, 1952, he reminisced about its creation and its service to the Chief Executive. He said:

" …Those of you who are deep in the Central Intelligence Agency know what goes on around the world; know what is necessary for the President to know every morning. I am briefed every day on all the world, on everything that takes place from one end of the world to the other, all the way around; by both the poles and the

" …Those of you who are deep in the Central Intelligence Agency know what goes on around the world; know what is necessary for the President to know every morning. I am briefed every day on all the world, on everything that takes place from one end of the world to the other, all the way around; by both the poles and the other way. It is necessary that you make that contribution for the welfare and benefit of your government.

President Dwight D. Eisenhower

other way. It is necessary that you make that contribution for the welfare and benefit of your government.

"I came over here to tell you how appreciative I am of the service which I have received as the Chief Executive of the greatest nation in the history of the world."

President Dwight D. Eisenhower appointed Allen W. Dulles Director of Central Intelligence. Dulles was sworn in on February 26, five weeks after Eisenhower took the presidential oath. This began the "Dulles Decade" at the Central Intelligence Agency.

Creating a headquarters on a suitable piece of federal land close enough to be effective was the solution to the problem of crowded and inefficient office space for the CIA. Allen Dulles advocated such a course of action. President Eisenhower and Congress agreed. On August 4, 1955, President Eisenhower signed the bill that authorized $46 million for construction of a CIA Headquarters Building.

With that action, the end of the tenure of the CIA at the E Street Complex and elsewhere downtown was in sight. Most of the people of the Agency would leave the archaic buildings and move into a modern new building. First, however, the site had to be found, and the building designed and constructed.

The site selected for the headquarters building was seven miles northwest of the White House on the Virginia side of the Potomac River. ●

Left **Building Q was on the south side of the Capitol Mall near Building M, within easy walking distance of the main campus. It was one of several temporary wartime buildings that survived into the 1950s.**

Chapter Two

Moving to the Langley Campus

*The location selected for the CIA's headquarters is on a site above the Potomac River.
It lies on high ground on the right bank of the Virginia side of the river, seven miles
northwest of the White House and approximately two miles upstream from
Little Falls, the fall line in northeastern Fairfax County.*

Previous page, left **Vertical aerial photo defines the Langley site for the new CIA headquarters as site preparation begins. The Potomac River is above the site to the northeast. Residential area of northwest Washington, DC, is at the top across the river. Fairfax County, Virginia, embraces the site, with Langley and McLean as the nearest towns. The campus site comprises 258 acres.**

Previous page, right **Low oblique aerial photo of the CIA Headquarters site after construction began.**

Right **It is Tuesday and Election Day, November 3, 1959. The crowd awaits President Eisenhower's arrival for dedication of the Original Headquarters Building.**

History of the Langley Site

The Potomac River flows from headwaters in the Appalachian Mountains to the Chesapeake Bay, passing the capital city of Washington, DC, about fifty-five miles north of its confluence with the Bay at Point Lookout. In the ages of its existence, the Potomac has cut through soft soils and detoured around the resistance of hard rock. The river's path, seldom straight, is marked by turns and curves. The process of natural erosion over thousands of years has created long stretches of tranquil waters as well as perilous stretches of roaring rapids that can drown the careless or unwary. In some places, the banks are only a few feet above the water. In others, the river flows far beneath high bluffs.

Archeological records confirm that the earliest prehistoric occupation of the region dates back about eleven millennia. The area was suitable for settlement by the prehistoric Paleoindians because of its natural resources, such as deposits of quartz that the Paleoindians used to make stone tools and spear points. Also, inhabitants could grow or hunt natural food sources. Some game included prehistoric mammals that are now extinct. The Potomac River allowed convenient access to the diverse resources of both the river valley and piedmont uplands. Native Americans continued to inhabit that region of Fairfax County through colonial days.

When the British colonists came to the region, the land, including the CIA site, was part of a grant to Thomas Lee by the Proprietors of the Northern Neck. They granted Lee

When the British colonists came to the region, the land, including the CIA site, was part of a grant to Thomas Lee by the Proprietors of the Northern Neck. They granted Lee a tract of more than 2,800 acres of land in 1719. Lee's family estate in England was named Langley, and he chose the name for his new property. To this day, many people still use "Langley" when referring to CIA Headquarters.

a tract of more than 2,800 acres of land in 1719. Lee's family estate in England was named Langley, and he chose the name for his new property. To this day, many people still use "Langley" when referring to CIA Headquarters.

In later years, families named Reid, Green, and Cruickshank occupied the site. During the Civil War the site was along the chain of forts hurriedly constructed by Union forces on the heights around Washington in 1861 after the Confederate victory at Manassas in July. The forts were erected to repel Confederate forces if they attacked the capital city. Two of the fortifications, Camp Griffin and Camp Pierpoint, were constructed in the vicinity during the winter of 1861-62. Maj. Gen. George B. McClellan, commander of the Army of the Potomac, established his headquarters at Camp Griffin.

More than 20,000 Union troops occupied Camp Griffin, using it as winter quarters and as a training base. Camp Griffin was dismantled in March 1862, as the immediate Confederate threat subsided and troops were needed elsewhere.

Although the camp was dismantled, relics of that era remind us of the activity then. For example, during Camp Griffin's active period, an Army mule lost its shoe. This mule shoe was found at the site during excavations for the Agency's Original Headquarters Building.

Seven decades later, in 1938, the federal government acquired 465 acres of the land for the Federal Highway Administration (FHWA). The land was intended for a planned research campus. Although the administrative

Right **Allen W. Dulles told the audience at the laying of the Cornerstone for the Original Headquarters Building: "The law creating the Agency was voted by a Congress in which there was a Republican majority. It was sponsored and signed by a Democratic President. For the past crucial years it has had the unfailing support of a Republican President and a Democratic Congress. Facts have no politics." His term as Director of Central Intelligence was the longest of any since its establishment, from February 26, 1953, to November 29, 1961.**

building was completed in 1942, World War II deflected the larger FHWA plans, and the campus was never built. A small field laboratory on forty-three acres called the Turner Fairbanks Facility (Langley) tests roadside hardware and night vision products, and is developing a prototype of the "highway of the future."

Design and Construction

With the money authorized and appropriated and the land acquired, design and construction of the CIA's headquarters building began. The New York architectural firm

Right **President Eisenhower wields the trowel to spread mortar for the Cornerstone of the Original Headquarters Building. DCI Allen W. Dulles is visible over President Eisenhower's head. After the ceremony, President Eisenhower drove up the newly constructed extension of the George Washington Memorial Parkway, then boarded the VH-34 helicopter Marine One to fly to Gettysburg to vote. He was back at the White House by mid-afternoon.**

Opposite page **Col. Lawrence K. White, Deputy Director for Support, inserts a box with contemporary memorabilia into the Cornerstone. Historian Walter Pforzheimer watches. When members of the press asked DCI Dulles what was in the box, he replied with a grin, "It's a secret." Actually, contents of the box were itemized in the program for the event.**

Contents of the Cornerstone Box

During the dedication ceremony on November 3, 1959, a box of documents and other materials was sealed inside the Cornerstone of the Original Headquarters Building. The intent was to provide items of historic interest at some future date, when the box was opened.

After the ceremony, members of the media asked DCI Allen W. Dulles what was in the box. He grinned and said, "It's a secret." Here is a list of the items that repose in the sealed box inside the Cornerstone, as listed in the dedication program:

1 Memorandum for President Franklin D. Roosevelt from Maj. Gen. William J. Donovan, Director of the Office of Strategic Services, dated 18 November 1944, regarding the establishment of a permanent centralized intelligence service and Memorandum from President Roosevelt to General Donovan, dated 5 April 1944, directing that General Donovan discuss his plan with the appropriate officials of the Government.

2 President Harry S. Truman's Executive Letter of 22 January 1946, establishing the National Intelligence Authority and the Central Intelligence Group.

3 Statement of Gen. (then Lt. Gen.) Hoyt S. Vandenberg, Director of Central Intelligence, before the Senate Committee on Armed Services, on 29 April 1947, in support of the sections of the proposed National Security Act of 1947 to establish the Central Intelligence Agency.

4 A Text and Explanation of Statutes and Executive Orders relating specifically to the Central Intelligence Agency, including Enabling and Appropriations Acts for the construction of the new CIA building.

5 Reproduction of the CIA seal and its official description.

6 "William J. Donovan and the National Security." A speech by Allen W. Dulles, Director of Central Intelligence, to the Erie County Bar Association, Buffalo, New York, 4 May 1959.

7 An aerial photograph of the area of the CIA Building site.

8 Drawings of the CIA Building as it will appear when completed.

9 The Program, a recording, and photographs of the Cornerstone Ceremony.

10 Microfilm copies of daily and weekly newspapers of 3 November 1959.

Left **James Garrison, Director of Logistics, ensures that the time capsule box is in place as the Cornerstone of the Original Headquarters Building is lowered into place. Most of the "time capsule" box is obscured by the Cornerstone.**

of Wallace K. Harrison and Max Abramovitz was responsible for the design. Notable among their earlier design credits was the United Nations Building in New York.

Allen Dulles set forth the guiding principle for creation of the headquarters compound. The goal was to create a pastoral, campus-like setting that would attract the best and the brightest in the arena of international affairs, while also assuring visual privacy and physical security for the CIA's family of employees.

The Charles H. Tompkins Co. - J.A. Jones Construction Co. were the builders. Their task was to transform the Harrison and Abramovitz design of Allen Dulles's vision into high-quality office space and the ancillary uses necessary to support the administrative, analytical, and operational needs of the agency. Site preparation and construction began in October 1957. Precast concrete was the choice for the seven-story main structure.

The north and east edges of the complex are heavily wooded. About sixty percent remains undeveloped. The forty percent of the area that is natural forest cover is well-populated with deciduous and evergreen trees growing up to 200 feet into the sky. Dominant trees in the natural forest are the tulip poplar and red maple. Other trees that populate the area include white oak, sycamore, American beech, and mixed species of pines. Sassafras and paw-paw trees can be found along the lower elevations near stream channels. In autumn, the multiple colors of the deciduous leaves stand out against the constant green of the pines.

Smaller vegetation includes holly and dogwood, with stands of mountain laurel. The bright red berries of the

Opposite page **The pilot of Sam Whitt's Cessna 150 turned the airplane for him to provide this view of the Original Headquarters Building under construction in 1960. Photo courtesy Sam Whitt.**

holly provide colorful accents in the winter, while the flowers of the mountain laurel give splashes of color in May and June. Ground cover consists mainly of herbaceous perennials such as horsetail, wood ferns, and honeysuckle.

Extensive landscaping was done to the site during development. A stand of willow oaks grows along the entrance road. The main entrance to the Original Headquarters Building (OHB) is accented with saucer magnolias. Mature evergreens appear in small stands to the north and south of the OHB. Many ornamental shrubs were planted to enhance the site, including azaleas, rhododendrons, mountain laurel, and viburnums.

Access to the 219-acre site is off Virginia Route 123. The road is named Dolley Madison Boulevard west of the CIA and Chain Bridge Road east of it. The road passes along the southern edge of the CIA compound, traversing the nearby communities of McLean and Langley before dipping downhill to the Chain Bridge across the Potomac into Washington.

The George Washington Memorial Parkway was extended northwestward to allow access to the northern perimeter of the complex. The GW Parkway began near Mount Vernon and ran along the Virginia side of the Potomac through Alexandria and Arlington. The extension joined up with the Capital Beltway (I-495) on the Virginia side of the river, where the Cabin John (American Legion) Bridge was being finished. The Beltway was under construction then and was called the Circumferential Highway. An internal road looped from Virginia Route 123 on the

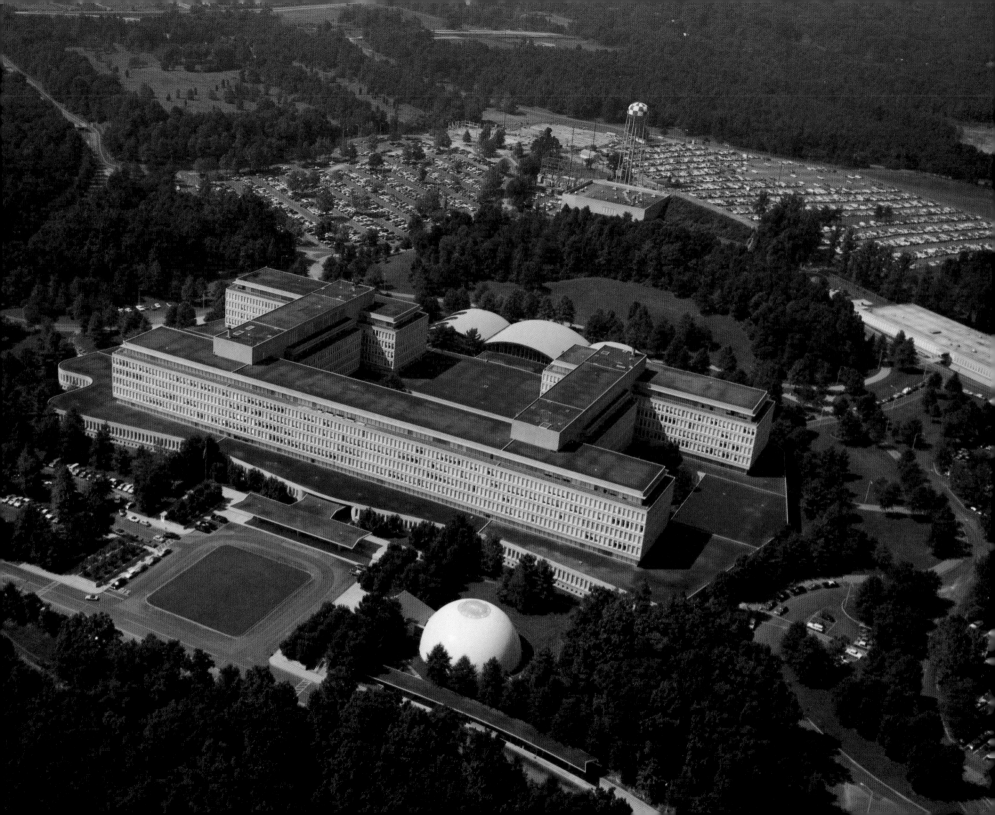

Right **For more than two decades beginning in the 1960s, this was the main entrance to the CIA campus. It was upgraded during the expansion in the mid-1980s.**

Left **Visitors take heed; cameras are prohibited. This admonition prevailed through the 1970s and 1980s. In the 1990s, the prohibitions were extended to video cameras, computers, and more.**

Right **A few parking spaces were provided near the front entrance to the Original Headquarters Building. A small VIP parking area is to the left of this photo. Horizontal sweep of the structure is apparent here, as are the many trees preserved during construction.**

south, past parking areas and support buildings, to the Original Headquarters Building, and onward to link up with the parkway extension. The long axis of the OHB is east-west oriented. Seen from above, the building resembles a large capital letter "H" with two crossbars. The double crossbars create an expansive courtyard in the center, and the westward vertical stroke of the "H" is open in the middle and gives access to the cafeteria. The building occupies about nine acres.

Presidential Visits

Construction progressed rapidly. Two years after the first work was completed, the Cornerstone Dedication Ceremony was held on the site, with participants seeing the seven-story building beginning to rise upward from its base.

The Chaplain of the United States Senate, Rev. Frederick Brown Harris, delivered the invocation. In his principal presentation, President Dwight D. Eisenhower spoke about the need for intelligence in national affairs. He was a keen customer for intelligence, who used it in planning and decision-making as Supreme Allied Commander in Europe during WW II. His appreciation for intelligence remained high during his two presidential terms. The Korean War ended in 1953 during his tenure, the Suez Crisis and Soviet crushing of the Hungarian Revolution blew up in October 1956, and Fidel Castro brought Communist rule to Cuba in 1959-60, while President Eisenhower served in the White House.

"America's fundamental aspiration is the preservation of peace. To this end we seek to develop policies and arrangements to make the peace both permanent and just. This can be done only on the basis of comprehensive and appropriate information."

President Dwight D. Eisenhower

"If they [our beliefs] be sound and enduring, based on the deep moral strivings of man and the highest conception of our national interests, let us cling to them. But in the field of our relations with our fellowmen abroad, let us assure ourselves, through accurate intelligence, that our attachments to policies are soundly based."

Director Allen W. Dulles

Key points from his remarks remain pertinent and timeless nearly four decades later. He said:

"America's fundamental aspiration is the preservation of peace. To this end we seek to develop policies and arrangements to make the peace both permanent and just. This can be done only on the basis of comprehensive and appropriate information.

"In war nothing is more important to a commander than the facts concerning the strength, dispositions, and intentions of his opponent, and the proper interpretation of those facts. In peacetime the necessary facts are of a different nature. They deal with conditions, resources, requirements, and attitudes prevailing in the world. They and their correct interpretation are essential to the development of policy to further our long term national security and best interests. To provide information of this kind is the task of the organization of which you are a part.

"No task could be more important.

"Upon the quality of your work depends in large measure the success of our effort to further the Nation's position in the international scene."

He mentioned the dedication and selflessness of persons who pursued careers in intelligence and concluded by saying: "I deem it a great privilege to participate in this ceremony of Cornerstone laying for the national headquarters of the Central Intelligence Agency. On this spot will rise a beautiful and a useful structure. May it long endure, to serve the cause of America and of peace."

Director Allen W. Dulles followed President Eisenhower at the microphone. He remarked upon the perils of the

Left **Bus stop along the loop road in the 1960s. Auditorium and Original Headquarters Building are in the background.**

Right **Early expansion. The need to support the weight of heavy printing presses and to provide secure space for printing activities led to construction of a separate building. This is the site for the Printing Services Division building under preparation in 1966. It sits down the hill west of the headquarters buildings. The name of the building is now the Printing and Photography Building.**

postwar world, in locations that soon would be known to all Americans. Here are extracts from his speech:

"World War II and its aftermath and the international communist threat had already brought home to us that our vital interests were at stake in places as distant as Korea, and Laos, in Africa, and the Islands of the Pacific, as well as in this Hemisphere and in Europe."

Dulles also described the bipartisan nature of support for the creation of the headquarters: "The law creating the Agency was voted by a Congress in which there was a Republican majority. It was sponsored and signed by a Democratic President. For the past crucial years it has had the unfailing support of a Republican President and a Democratic Congress. Facts have no politics."

He concluded with his thoughts on the need for the CIA to seek the truth. They provide sound guidance for intelligence professionals, and also for the rest of us: "If they [our beliefs] be sound and enduring, based on the deep moral strivings of man and the highest conception of our national interests, let us cling to them. But in the field of our relations with our fellowmen abroad, let us assure ourselves, through accurate intelligence, that our attachments to policies are soundly based.

"It is the particular duty of this Agency to help perform this function in a world where change is the rule rather than the exception. This task must be carried out fearlessly, without warping to meet our prejudices or our predilections or even the tenets of existing policy.

"As we build a new edifice in which to house, to concentrate and coordinate our work, we must rededicate ourselves to this high purpose.

"The guiding motto to be inscribed on the face of this building will be the words taken from the Gospel according to St. John: 'Ye shall know the truth, and the truth shall make you free.'"

The first of the CIA employees moved into the Original Headquarters Building on September 20, 1961. By then the building's north half, cafeteria, and parking areas were ready. The persons in Buildings M and Q near the Tidal Basin were the first to leave downtown.

Construction continued until the building's completion in November 1963. Employees enjoyed much more space, and more comfortable and functional space, than they were accustomed to in the old E Street Complex. The new building included 1.4 million square feet of office space, along with bright cafeteria space with the capacity to seat 1,500. The gymnasium contained a one-tenth mile indoor track. The courtyards and modern meeting space in the Headquarters Auditorium (nicknamed "the Bubble") next to the OHB added to the amenities.

The complex lived up to the principles expressed by the CIA in its planning. It now had a first-class location for first-class people to produce equally top-quality intelligence in the national interest. During the shift from downtown to the new Langley headquarters, President John F. Kennedy visited. The CIA played prominent roles in two major crises of Kennedy's short presidential term. The April 1961 invasion of Cuba at the Bay of Pigs had already occurred,

Right **Allen W. Dulles (center) introduces President Kennedy to visitors after receiving the National Security Medal.**

and the Cuban missile crisis of October 1962 was eleven months in the future when Kennedy visited the new CIA headquarters on November 28, 1961.

DCI Allen W. Dulles was eased out in the delayed fallout from the Bay of Pigs invasion. He was awarded the National Security Medal by President Kennedy and retired. John A. McCone succeeded Allen Dulles on November 29, 1961, and served as Director of Central Intelligence until April 28, 1965.

Less than a year after John McCone succeeded Dulles, President Kennedy was embroiled in the Cuban Missile Crisis. The CIA shone brightly in that crisis, enabling Kennedy to prevail.

President Harry S. Truman, who signed the legislation creating the CIA, paid tribute to it during his retirement. On June 9, 1964, he presented the Agency with his photograph, inscribed thus:

"To the Central Intelligence Agency, a necessity to the President of the United States, from one who knows." — Harry S. Truman.

By the time President Truman wrote those words the Original Headquarters Building was completed. Follow the tour up the steps of the building to view the interior. ●

Chapter Three

Inside the Original Headquarters Building

Public tours of the CIA campus and its buildings are not conducted. Logistical and security considerations prevent such tours. Therefore, the material in this book enables the reader to enjoy the experience as a tour of the complex.

Previous page, left **Passing through the entrance doors, one immediately encounters the CIA Seal set into the floor. Seen up close, the American Eagle projects strength and alertness, and the radiating spokes of the compass rose indeed seem to reach out everywhere to gather data and bring it here. Standing here and looking to the left one sees high on the wall the quotation from the Bible, "Ye shall know the truth and the truth shall make you free" (John XIII-XXXII). General Donovan's statue is also on the left. On the right side of the foyer is the Memorial Wall.**

Previous page, right **A visitor to the Central Intelligence Agency mounts these steps to enter the front entrance of the Original Headquarters Building (OHB). Parking near this entrance is quite limited. Most CIA personnel enter the buildings via several other entrances nearer the parking areas.**

Next stop on the surrogate tour begins at the front steps of the Original Headquarters Building, on the east side. To fully appreciate the building, it is important to understand its general layout.

The ground and first floors constitute an oblong base with curved outer walls and corners, enclosing three landscaped courtyards. The two side courtyards are 80 feet by 140 feet, and the center court measures 260 feet by 140 feet.

Consider the facade of the building. Architectural features include a setback at the second floor and another at the seventh floor. Continuous glass windows form the exterior walls of these two floors. The ground floor has small windows set rather high above the floor level every five feet. The remaining five floors have windows approximately three feet wide by seven feet high, also spaced five feet apart. The windows of these five floors are set in pre-cast concrete with a quartz aggregate finish that provides a sparkling and refreshing contrast to the regular concrete of the ground floor.

The building looks inviting from outside, with the brightness of the hundreds of vertical windows contrasting with the long horizontal lines of the floor levels. Adm. Stansfield Turner, USN, who was Director of Central Intelligence from March 9, 1977, to January 20, 1981, called it "anything but sinister."

The long axis of the building, which runs north to south, is 926 feet long, and the width (east to west) measures 475 feet, excluding the cafeteria. Rising from this two-story base are five connected towers 90 feet wide and

Left **A CIA employee greeting a visitor in the 1960s through 1980s would have this view as the visitor approached from the CIA Seal toward the security post in the center. This photo was taken in autumn, during Fire Prevention Week.**

varying in length from 150 feet to 670 feet. These towers contain six floors, numbered two through seven.

Entering the Building

The main entrance is one of several into the building. From a position facing the entrance, the Headquarters Auditorium, with its distinctive hemispheric shape, is situated to the right (north).

An American flag ripples in the breeze to the left (south). The flagpole reaches almost to the height of the fourth floor of the building. The front doors to the building are reached from the quadrangle's ground level via low-rise steps or a convenient ramp. The first-time visitor who passes through the door cannot help but be impressed by the spaciousness and light. The CIA Seal is set into the floor directly in front of persons entering. Square vertical columns spaced twenty feet apart lead the eye upward to the high ceiling. In the golden anniversary year of 1997, CIA50 banners hang from each of the columns in the entrance foyer.

A biblical verse is etched into the left (south) wall high up near the ceiling. It characterizes the intelligence mission and reflects Allen Dulles's remarks at the dedication of the building's cornerstone: "Ye shall know the truth and the truth shall make you free" (John VIII-XXXII).

Beneath the inscription is the OSS Memorial with its Book of Honor and a life-size statue of General Donovan. On the right side is the north wall. A bas-relief bust of Allen W. Dulles is displayed there. The major feature here is the Memorial Wall. Stars carved into the marble facade

Opposite Page **Portrait of Maj. Gen. William J. Donovan (left) is encountered first in this "DCI Hallway" on the first floor of the OHB. His successors appear in order of service proceeding down the hall, with Rear Adm. Sidney W. Souers, USNR, and Lt. Gen. Hoyt S. Vandenberg, USA, next.**

Opposite page **The DCI Hallway from the other end. The most recent oil portrait in the hallway is of R. James Woolsey, (on the right in this mid-1997 photo) DCI from February 5, 1993, to January 10, 1995. Next on the left is the portrait of Robert M. Gates, DCI from November 6, 1991, through January 19, 1993.**

immortalize those who lost their lives while serving their country in the field of intelligence.

From the entrance foyer, a visitor next encounters the security checkpoint. A sign reminds all visitors of the items prohibited inside of the building. They include firearms and ammunition, explosives and incendiary devices, cameras and photographic equipment, transmitting and receiving equipment, alcoholic beverages and narcotics, and animals other than guide dogs. Disturbances, the solicitation or distribution of handbills, gambling, and smoking in non-designated areas are all prohibited activities.

Hallways and Amenities

After the visitor is admitted through the security checkpoint, a cleared CIA employee escorts the visitor into the building. The hallways are wide, quiet, and sparkling clean. The hallway on the south side of the first floor is decorated with portraits of Directors of Central Intelligence. One first encounters General Donovan's portrait, followed by others in chronological order from east to west down the hall.

The working offices are conventional and well-lighted by both natural and electric light. Interior masonry walls are generally painted plaster. Most of the interior partitioning that divides and subdivides internal office spaces is made of steel. The partitions are moveable so that space can be adapted to changing requirements. Full height partitioning is floor to ceiling, and partial height partitioning is from the floor to sixty-eight inches high. The cafeteria is nestled along the western edge of the Original

Headquarters Building, easily reached from all parts. Its design illustrates success in realizing the principles desired for the CIA campus. Its arched, curved structure is a contrast to the horizontal and vertical lines of the Original Headquarters Building.

Entering the cafeteria, one feels the transition from a working environment to a dining area, and it is welcome. Like the OHB, the cafeteria structure is filled with an abundance of natural light. Its ground-level location and the expanses of glass on all sides and above enable diners to take in the vistas of forest, landscaped courtyards, and the ever-changing scenery of the sky.

The cafeteria is situated between the Original Headquarters Building and its companion, the New Headquarters Building. The construction of the NHB began in May 1984. The story of the New Headquarters Building is told in Chapter Five. For now, the tour will visit one more area in the Original Headquarters Building.

CIA employees can shop at the "Company Store," which is close to the cafeteria. The Employee Activity Association (EAA) operates the store. In addition to carrying a range of convenience and necessity items, the store stocks quality merchandise with the CIA logo. In observance of the CIA's golden anniversary, CIA50 items are available for purchase in 1997.

The Employee Activity Association completed its thirty-third year of operation in 1997. It is a nonprofit Virginia corporation dedicated to improving the quality of life for CIA employees. EAA offers members a range of features that includes the opportunity to join a variety of social,

Right **The Operations Center is the nerve center and focal point for U.S. intelligence activities. It is similar to the White House Situation Room and National Military Command Center in the Pentagon. It is staffed around the clock every day of the year.**

Left **On the first floor of the Original Headquarters Building is the main reading room of the CIA research library. Open to Agency personnel only, its holdings include more than 125,000 volumes and 1,700 serials. This photo was taken in the 1960s. The massive card catalog is on the left.**

Opposite page **Inside the Headquarters Auditorium in the 1960s. Also called "the Bubble," where senior CIA leadership holds ceremonies, presentations, and town meetings. Its area encompasses 7,000 square feet, including stage and seating for 500 persons. Listening devices are available for persons who are hearing impaired. Wheelchair access is provided.**

educational, recreational, health, and self-improvement clubs and groups. Also, the EAA offers year-round intramural sports programs as well as extensive entertainment event ticketing and film processing services. EAA members may also make personal travel arrangements and take advantage of car buying and discount merchandise programs.

Mention of the EAA's Company Store is a natural lead-in to considering the CIA's place in the economic structure of Fairfax County, Virginia. When the CIA moved from the E Street Complex to Langley beginning in 1961, the suburban surge in the greater Washington area was in its infancy. Overnight the CIA became one of Fairfax County's largest employers. The thousands of CIA employees occupying an office building with 1.4 million square feet of space had a major impact on economic activity in northeastern Fairfax County. Nearby communities such as McLean and Langley prospered and grew, both as residential areas and also in the commercial sphere.

By 1973, a dozen years after the CIA moved in, Fairfax County's business base had expanded. In that year it counted 847 major businesses on its rolls, occupying 11.7 million square feet under roof. That count did not include the office space of federal government activities such as the CIA.

Presidential Visits

The Director of Central Intelligence is the primary advisor to the President and the National Security Council on intelligence matters. Most presidents since Harry Truman

Opposite page **Main reading room of the CIA research library in 1997. In addition to the extensive book and periodical collections, materials are also available on CD-ROM, and are accessible via thousands of commercial database files. The library contains the Historical Intelligence Collection with more than 23,000 books and thousands of press clippings on the intelligence profession.**

have received global intelligence briefings from CIA professionals at the White House in the early hours of their workdays.

From time to time, presidents have journeyed to the CIA headquarters for briefings, ceremonies, or other purposes to meet their requirements for conduct of the office. Just as their predecessors did, a succession of presidents in the 1960s and 1970s expressed their admiration for the superb work of the CIA professionals of all disciplines.

President Lyndon B. Johnson took office after President Kennedy's assassination on November 22, 1963. Although he wanted to focus on domestic programs via his Great Society, world events required much of President Johnson's attention. The CIA gave him full attention and support in situations such as the intervention in the Dominican Republic in 1965, the war in Vietnam, and continued tensions with the Soviet Union.

President Johnson visited the headquarters on April 28, 1965. The purpose of his visit was to swear in the new Director of Central Intelligence and the Deputy Director of Intelligence (DDCI). Vice Adm. William F. Raborn Jr., USN (Ret.), succeeded John McCone as DCI. Richard Helms took the oath as DDCI in the same ceremony.

In his remarks at the double oath-taking ceremony, President Johnson said:

" …We have committed our lives, our property, our resources, and our sacred honor to the freedom and peace of other men, indeed to the freedom and peace of all mankind. We would dishonor that commitment, we would

Right **At any time of day or night, or season of the year, the cafeteria provides a relaxing contrast to the high intensity of the working offices.**

disgrace all the sacrifices that Americans have made if we were not every hour of every day vigilant against every threat to peace and freedom. That is why we have the Central Intelligence Agency in this country."

A note is in order on the special status of the Deputy Director. In the earliest days of the CIA, the DCI appointed the Deputy Director. That was changed in April 1953, when Congress amended the National Security Act of 1947. According to the amended act, the president was required to appoint the DDCI with the advice and consent of the Senate. Also, the amendment prohibited commis-

Right **Cafeteria, with courtyard vista.**

Opposite page **Agency employees are able to shop at the "Company Store" operated by the Employee Activity Association (EAA). The EAA is a nonprofit Virginia corporation dedicated to improving the quality of life for CIA employees. Merchandise bearing the CIA logo became available in the 1990s, and a special line of CIA fiftieth anniversary items was added in 1997. The EAA observed its thirty-third year of operation in 1997.**

Right **The Blue Bird Body Company headquarters is in Fort Valley, Georgia. The company produces school buses and "flat front" buses like this one used in the CIA shuttle bus fleet for decades.**

sioned officers of the armed forces from occupying both the DCI and DDCI positions at the same time. This applies whether the officers are active or retired.

Before the 1953 amendment, two commissioned officers had served simultaneously in the DCI and DDCI posts one time. The period was from May 1, 1947, through March 9, 1949, while Rear Adm. Roscoe H. Hillenkoetter, USN, was DCI and Brig. Gen. Edwin K. Wright, USA, was Deputy

DCI. In all other instances either the DCI or DDCI was a civilian, or both were civilians.

When Admiral Raborn retired a year after taking his oath, on June 30, 1966, President Johnson returned to the CIA headquarters to promote Richard Helms to the position of Director of Central Intelligence. Helms served in the post for nearly seven years, until February 2, 1973.

In his remarks on that occasion, President Johnson alluded to the elements of the intelligence cycle that

Right President Lyndon B. Johnson (on left) presides at the oath-taking by Vice Adm. William F. Raborn (on Johnson's left) as DCI and Richard W. Helms (center) as Deputy Director, on April 28, 1965. Admiral Raborn served as DCI until June 30, 1966. Mr. Helms succeeded him on that date and served until February 2, 1973.

include gathering of raw data and analyzing and converting it into finished intelligence. Referring to the persons who perform those tasks, he said, "In a real sense they are America's professional students; they are unsung, just as they are invaluable."

President Nixon defeated Hubert Humphrey in the election of 1968. Humphrey had been Lyndon Johnson's vice president and had visited the CIA during his time in office. Foreign policy was Nixon's strong suit, buttressed by his eight years as Dwight Eisenhower's vice president. President Nixon was initially cool to the CIA. However, as president he soon came to appreciate the Agency's service in dealing with the end to American involvement in the Vietnam War, his initiative in opening up relations with the People's Republic of China, and in handling the Strategic Arms Limitations Talks (SALT).

President Nixon expressed his thoughts on the role of the CIA during a visit to the Agency on March 7, 1969. He said: "I look upon this organization as not one that is necessary for the conduct of conflict or war, or call it what you may, but in the final analysis as one of the great instruments of our government for the preservation of peace, for the avoidance of war, and for the development of a society in which this kind of activity would not be necessary, if necessary at all."

When Richard Helms retired on February 2, 1973, James R. Schlesinger became Director of Central Intelligence under President Nixon. He served for five months. William E. Colby became DCI on September 4, 1973, serving under both Presidents Nixon and Ford.

"General Douglas MacArthur once said that in war there is no substitute for victory. Let me assure you that in peace there is no substitute for intelligence."

President Gerald R. Ford

Gerald R. Ford became president when President Nixon resigned office on August 8, 1974. He was the fourth consecutive president to have served in the Navy. Harry S. Truman and Dwight D. Eisenhower both served in the Army, and Franklin D. Roosevelt was Assistant Secretary of the Navy in World War I.

Gerald Ford knew more than most members of Congress about the intelligence business because of his service as a member of the intelligence appropriations sub-committee in the House of Representatives. Congressional scrutiny of the CIA intensified during his two and one-half years in office, most notably during the hearings conducted by Senator Frank Church (D-Idaho) in 1975. Amid the controversy he valued the service of the CIA in dealing with crises such as the fall of Saigon in April 1975.

President Ford voiced his concerns about the impulses in Congress to dismantle the intelligence systems. In his State of the Union address on January 19, 1976, he said:

" ...The crippling of our foreign intelligence services increases the danger of American involvement in direct armed conflict. Our adversaries are encouraged to attempt new adventures while our own ability to monitor events and to influence events short of military action is under-mined. Without effective intelligence capability, the United States stands blindfolded and hobbled."

Eleven days after his address, President Ford went out to the CIA to swear in George W. Bush as Director of Central Intelligence. Supreme Court Justice Potter Stewart administered the oath. Mrs. Barbara Bush held the Bible for her husband. President Ford continued to voice his

Left **DCI Richard W. Helms (left) escorts Vice President Hubert H. Humphrey (right) out of the Original Headquarters Building after the vice president visited the Langley headquarters.**

conviction of the value of intelligence for the nation. He said, "General Douglas MacArthur once said that in war there is no substitute for victory. Let me assure you that in peace there is no substitute for intelligence."

George Bush served as DCI until Jimmy Carter's inauguration as president on January 20, 1977. President Carter was the fifth successive president with U.S. Navy service. He chose Adm. Stansfield Turner, USN, a fellow member of the Class of 1946 at the U.S. Naval Academy, as his DCI.

President Carter and Admiral Turner redefined the relationship between Congress and the intelligence community. This resulted in more explicit guidance to the several intelligence organizations of the government and giving the DCI greater control of budget and assigning tasks for intelligence collection.

President Carter swore in Admiral Turner on March 9, little more than six weeks after his inauguration. Two weeks before, at the Department of State, President Carter emphasized the necessity of having an effective intelligence organization in peacetime:

"We sometimes relax too much in peacetime. We've got to establish this relationship [a good intelligence system] on a permanent, workable basis while we are at peace. It's one of the best means to make sure we don't have war. And if we should ever be in danger in a time of crisis, it's too late to build up an adequate intelligence community, including our worldwide system of information."

The CIA gave President Carter extensive support in two major international crises in 1979: the Soviet invasion of

Opposite page **President Richard M. Nixon and DCI Richard Helms during the president's visit to CIA headquarters, March 7, 1969.**

Right **Mrs. Barbara Bush (left) holds the Bible for George Bush to take the oath as DCI. Justice Potter Stewart swore in Mr. Bush. President Gerald Ford is on the right. Mr. Bush entered the directorship after being chief of the U.S. liaison office in Beijing, China, from October 1974 to December 1975. He served as DCI from January 30, 1976, until January 20, 1977.**

Afghanistan and the seizure of the American Embassy in Tehran, Iran, by Islamic militants.

The embassy in Tehran and its staff members were held hostage for 444 days. During their ordeal the 1980 elections in the United States resulted in the election of Ronald W. Reagan as president, with George W. Bush as his vice president. Admiral Turner stepped down as DCI on January 20, 1981, Inauguration Day for Ronald Reagan's first term. Reagan appointed William J. Casey as the Director of Central Intelligence. Casey had served in the OSS under General Donovan. His service included coordinating French Resistance forces in support of the Normandy invasion and liberation of France, and as chief of American intelligence operations in Europe.

The role of the intelligence services in the Reagan era required intensified activities and closer coordination. During his first term, plans were made for expansion of the Langley headquarters, and ground was broken for the New Headquarters Building. ●

Opposite page **President Jimmy Carter (left) arrives at CIA and is greeted by Adm. Stansfield Turner, USN, at the steps to the Original Headquarters Building. The date was March 7, 1977. The occasion was Admiral Turner's swearing-in as DCI.**

Left **Awards ceremonies are held in this room on the first floor of the Original Headquarters Building. The highest award is the Distinguished Intelligence Cross, "for a voluntary act or acts of extraordinary heroism involving the acceptance of existing dangers with conspicuous fortitude and exemplary courage."**

Chapter Four

Art and Exhibits

*Artwork graces the entrances and hallways of both the Original and the
New Headquarters Building and the grounds of the campus. Some items are
permanently displayed, such as the portraits along the DCI Hallway and the original
works by artists of the Washington Color School. Others are on temporary display, as part
of exhibits featured from time to time around a selected theme. In addition, geopolitical
exhibits showcase pieces of art and artifacts from several regions of the world.*

Previous page, left **The CIA's Fine Arts Commission is responsible for supervision and display of the artworks of the Melzac Collection in both buildings. This photo shows several pieces hung on the second floor of the NHB Atrium near the escalators. In the background on the left is Thomas Downing's *Center Grid*. Closest to the viewer on the right is Norman Bluhm's *Inside Orange*. The Fine Arts Commission provides commentary on each of the works in succeeding photos.**

Previous page, right **Inside Orange by Norman Bluhm, c. 1966. 72"W X 84"H. This is the latest of the Agency's three paintings by Bluhm. By this time in his career he was producing very open kinds of compositions. He enjoyed creating a "choreography" of color in his work, strong shapes forming paths of color along which the eye is drawn. One critic has suggested that Bluhm's study of architecture and his experience as a pilot influenced his paintings. They have a strong sense of structure but also a sense of infinite space. In comparison with his earlier canvases on the third floor, in this work the contrasts of color and value are heightened, and there is tension between the strong, inward-turning forms and the open light areas. Even with the structural sense shown, Bluhm still appears to enjoy the contribution of accidental drips and splashes to the final effect.**

Whatever its location or medium or source, the presence of art enriches the everyday working life of CIA employees.

The Fine Arts Commission of the CIA is responsible for acquiring and displaying art in the Agency's buildings and grounds, among its other duties. The Fine Arts Commission advises the Director of Central Intelligence and the Executive Director of the Central Intelligence Agency on esthetic matters relating to the Agency work environment within the Washington area.

The Commission was founded in the 1960s. Its members are chosen based on their interest, artistic background, representation from the various directorates of the Agency, and willingness to donate their time.

The Melzac Collection

Among the distinctive accomplishments of the Commission is arranging the loan of art from the Vincent Melzac Collection and displaying it in the buildings. Also, the Fine Arts Commission manages a program of exhibits that changes monthly. They are displayed in two locations: on the first floor of the OHB near the Office of Medical Services and in the NHB Atrium.

The Commission also arranges for portraits of the Directors of Central Intelligence and for loan of art from the Corcoran Gallery for display in the DCI office suite.

Major sculptures and memorials also fall within the scope of the Fine Arts Commission. Examples include

Left **Center Grid**, by Thomas Downing, 1960. 70"W X 70"H. In an earlier work (*Dapple*, 1959, #9 on second floor of NHB), Downing made use of a module of pure color to create a field of pulsating color cross the canvas surface. In *Center Grid* Downing uses the same module but is aiming for an entirely different effect. Now he marshals the color modules formally, and the play in space results from contrasts of focus and overlapping layers of depth. Downing saw himself as somewhat of a romantic: "I liked the feeling of my brush going around when I painted. Then I found out a remarkable thing about color; that it can move while being still." He used the objective structure of the painting as a neutral framework that would allow the color to operate in freedom. He said, "I use variations of color as a language." Downing's later adventures in color on shaped canvases are on the first floor.

commissioning and planning of the *Kryptos* sculpture by James Sanborn, the Berlin Wall Memorial, the OSS Memorial, the Memorial Wall, and the Memorial Garden. Those items are covered in Chapters Six and Seven. The original paintings that catch one's eye and interest along the hallways of both buildings were painted in the 1950s and 1960s era by artists from the Washington Color School. Vincent Melzac collected the paintings. He was a businessman, art patron, and former director of the Corcoran Gallery of Art in Washington, DC. From 1971 until his death in 1989, Mr. Melzac loaned artworks to the Agency. He also gave the bronze bust of President Bush that is displayed on the first floor of the OHB.

Vincent Melzac was an art lover who could not afford the paintings of old masters. Instead, he collected paintings by young local artists. He once allegedly bought a room full of paintings from an artist who needed money. He built an extensive network of known and emerging artists. The pieces from the Melzac Collection are representative examples of the Washington Color School, a part of post-World War II American modernism. According to the Fine Arts Commission, the lineage of the Washington Color School began in the burst of creativity after the end of World War II. Artists began expressing themselves by filling large canvases with color and non-representational shapes.

These artists called themselves abstract expressionists. Scorning realism, which they called "illusion," they focused on themselves—their personalities and states of mind—and on the materials and processes of painting. Working

Opposite page, **Mars Reflection, by Alma Thomas, 1972. 54"W X 70"H. Thomas is perhaps the most interesting figure, a matriarchal presence, of the Washington Color School painters. An African-American who lived all her life in the family house on 15th Street, she was an art teacher in the District of Columbia school system. After retiring in 1960, she devoted herself to art, doing all her paintings on her kitchen table. Her work reflects an interest in nature: the way light is reflected, the rhythms of color. Intrigued by the lunar landing in 1969, she did a series of "space paintings." Mars Reflection is a good example of why Thomas's paintings are often described in musical terms. She started with the blue as an undercoat and added the many subtly varied shades of red above it, using a blunt brush no wider than half an inch. This technique allows for a composition of spatial rhythm and harmony, as the ripples of color recede and advance regularly across the picture plane.**

Opposite page **Untitled work by Howard Mehring, c. 1958. 53"W X 36"H. Mehring presents a contrast here of pigment on the surface of the canvas with that of deep staining. The viscosity of the white areas, which is here virtually poured straight onto the canvas out of a bucket, is in vivid contrast to the thin ethereal space of the purple area, which appears to be poured and then blotted, resulting in deep staining. In some ways this work is reminiscent of a galaxy formation or of something biological, viewed under a microscope. This relationship to science is viewed as a very American characteristic of the artists of this period.**

over their canvases in many layers of color, they emphasized the action of painting, the manual gesture in the streaks, angles, and intensity of their brushwork. Abstract expressionist paintings in CIA Headquarters include Norman Bluhm's *Passing Waterfall* and *French—75* and two of Howard Mehring's works. They are displayed on the second floor of the NHB.

Papers of the Fine Arts Commission explain how the abstract expressionist movement evolved into the Washington Color School. In the late 1950s, some of Vincent Melzac's artist friends grew tired of the expressionist approach. They attempted to remove themselves from their work. This detachment extended even to their personalities and painting techniques.

Artists of this new school focused on color as having its own kind of meaning. Mentioning "the irrational, often emotional, effect of color," they tried to avoid lines and shapes that anyone could interpret as images. To remove the hand of the artist they used transparent washes, sometimes actually poured, to stain the canvas in unpredictable ways. Experimenting with optical effects—"what the eye can touch"—they reached for space and light with floating lines and pools of color.

The Fine Arts Commission stresses that these quintessentially Color School works do not depend on photographic representation or conceptual meaning for their impact, but on face-to-face encounters with simple color and texture. They are more about how color vibrates in the eye than about how it occupies the surface of the canvas.

Some of the Washington artists moved on to test simpli-

fied formats such as ribbons or circles of intense color. Examples cited by the Fine Arts Commission include Gene Davis's *Black Rhythm* and Thomas Downing's *Center Grid*.

The Fine Arts Commission notes that the art of the Melzac Collection is especially suitable for display around the CIA. The Washington Color School developed at the same time that the Original Headquarters Building was conceived and occupied in the late 1950s and early 1960s.

The size of the pieces (some as large as seven feet in the major dimension) makes them exceptionally well-suited to the massive structure of the headquarters buildings. The Fine Arts Commission selects locations for the paintings with Agency employees and their movement patterns in mind. The placement of the paintings enables employees to view the art from long distances down the corridors and from various angles, as when going up or down the escalators in the Atrium of the NHB. The varying natural lighting in the NHB enhances the dramatic appeal of the artwork.

The CIA Exhibit Center

The Exhibit Center is inside the New Headquarters Building. Its location in the Atrium enables a wash of natural light to shine through the broad expanse of glass overhead.

The collection is unique. The items on display, all authentic, were donated by the offices or persons who used them. The collection exhibits artifacts documenting

Opposite page **Untitled work by Howard Mehring, c. 1958. 77"W X 76"H. The subtle, yet at times striking, colors and the strong diagonal of the composition carry the viewer's eye across the canvas surface. Mehring used a new medium developed in the early 1950s called magna. Unlike water-based acrylic (also a product of the 1950s) magna is based on turpentine and mineral spirits. Applied directly onto the cotton canvas, it literally bites into the threads. There are as many as ten layers of magna paint "poured" onto the surface here, starting with the splash of orange and followed by layers of purple and violet and some subtle greens on top. Even as the paint is layered, the colors are not muddied, because the magna paint does not bleed into the successive layers of color. The composition is guided but not preconceived. The artist guides the paint as it is being poured across the canvas placed on the floor. Such a technique makes it impossible to control exactly how the colors will combine or be absorbed into the canvas fibers. The artist exerts some control through the amount of turpentine used to thin the paint, the amount of paint used, and the direction of paint flow. By allowing the chance occurrences to be incorporated into the work, Mehring creates a composition of particular liveliness and spontaneity.**

Right **Black Rhythm** by Gene Davis, c. 1964. 85"W X 90"H. This is the Agency's only work by Davis, one of the most noted of the Washington Color School artists. In a conscious effort to "purify" his work, he reduced painting to the fewest possible elements: stripes of equal width. He felt that this matrix allowed him to emphasize color orchestration, saying: "I paint by eye as a jazz musician plays by ear." The stripes, like a drummer's beat, provide the unity through which the colors interact. Such a painting cannot be grasped all at once. Davis suggested that the viewer follow one color across the composition, seeing how the intervals work and what the rhythms are like between related colors. He described it as a kind of syncopation. A Washington native, Davis was a sports writer and a White House correspondent before he left that career to become a painter.

Right **Entrance to the CIA Exhibit Center in the New Headquarters Building. On the far wall is the first American flag to fly over the Headquarters compound. A chunk of the Berlin Wall rests on the floor in front of it.**

the role of intelligence in American history.

Maj. Gen. William J. Donovan, wartime head of the Office of Strategic Services, is represented in the collection by items of personal clothing and equipment. The desk and the maps that he used at the E Street Complex during the OSS days are on display. Gadgets and equipment from World War II include the German "Enigma" encoding machine and caltrops (tire spikes) used to harass enemy vehicle traffic. Caltrops have four spikes. When thrown on the ground, one of the spikes always points upward to pierce a tire or a shoe. Allen W. Dulles, who conducted intelligence activities from Bern, Switzerland, during WW II with the OSS, contributed a bust of Herman Goering, the head of Germany's Luftwaffe.

The first American flag to fly over the Headquarters compound graces one wall. Not far from it is one of the last American flags to fly over Checkpoint Charlie, one of the few locations for passage between West and East Berlin after the Berlin Wall was erected in 1961. When the Wall was torn down in 1989, a 300-pound chunk was saved for the CIA Exhibit Center. Other items of more recent vintage include psychological warfare leaflets created by the CIA during Operation Desert Storm. They were dropped over Iraqi target areas before Allied bombing raids. Civilians had time to evacuate the area, and the morale and resolve of the military units were weakened.

Items of spy tradecraft include a microdot camera, a .22 caliber gun cane, a hollow silver dollar for concealing microdots, a matchbox camera, and even a crossbow used by Montagnard tribesmen during the Vietnam War.

Gifts from foreign governments and dignitaries are displayed here also. So are letters, such as the one from Josef Stalin's daughter, Svetlana Alliluyeva, requesting political asylum and the opportunity to say good-bye to her children.

The Exhibit Center maintains pages on the CIA Web site on the Internet. There one can find photographs and descriptions of many of the relics in the collection.

The Exhibit Center is inside the New Headquarters Building. Its location in the Atrium enables a wash of natural light to shine through the broad expanse of glass overhead.

Opposite page **The first American flag to fly over the Headquarters compound is displayed on the far wall of this section of the Exhibit Center. In the glass case on the right are memorabilia of Maj. Gen. William J. Donovan. Among other artifacts on display are an encased 300-pound section of the Berlin Wall, a miniature camera, a hollowed-out Eisenhower dollar, dead-drop spike, and more.**

Left **A corner of the CIA Exhibit Center in the New Headquarters Building, with artifacts displayed in glass cases. Artifacts associated with the history of American intelligence activities are displayed here.**

Right **Inside the CIA Exhibit Center. A 300-pound chunk of the Berlin Wall is in the right corner in front of the first American flag to fly over the CIA headquarters compound.**

Left **Inside the CIA Exhibit Center. A curved desk made for former President George Bush when he served as DCI sits against the wall on the right. Mr. Bush never used the desk.**

In 1997, H. Keith Melton loaned his collection of intelligence artifacts to the CIA for display under guidance from the Fine Arts Commission. Melton is a well-known military historian and an expert on espionage paraphernalia. His collection includes a unique assortment of equipment used by Soviet and other services. The Fine Arts Commission placed the Melton Collection in the first floor exhibit hall of the Original Headquarters Building. ●

Opposite page **Maj. Gen. William J. Donovan wore this uniform jacket when he served as Director of the Office of Strategic Services during World War II. The garment was nicknamed the "Ike jacket" after General Dwight D. Eisenhower, Supreme Commander of Allied Forces in Europe, who sparked the design. The senior ribbon on the jacket is for the Medal of Honor, which General Donovan received for his gallantry and intrepidity above and beyond the call of duty during World War I as a combat leader of the legendary "Fighting 69th" Infantry. He was the most highly decorated officer from any country who fought in that war.**

Opposite page **DCI William J. Casey, himself a veteran of the Office of Strategic Services (OSS) during World War II, shows a wartime warning sign during an OSS reunion in the headquarters in 1986. Casey was DCI from January 28, 1981, through January 29, 1987.**

Chapter Five

Expansion and the New Headquarters Building

The need for expansion of the Langley campus was evident by the beginning of Ronald Reagan's presidency in 1981. More office space was required, as was parking space. The plans made in the 1950s for the complex provided for expansion beyond the Original Headquarters Building if necessary. Once the need was clear, the expansion process began.

Opposite page **Gentlemen, dig in! Groundbreaking ceremony for the headquarters expansion on May 8, 1984. In action from left to right are Rep. Frank R. Wolf (R-VA), Sen. John H. Chafee (R-RI), President Ronald W. Reagan, Vice President George W. Bush, DCI William J. Casey, and Deputy DCI John N. McMahon.**

Left **President Ronald W. Reagan applies foot to shovel, piercing the Virginia soil to break ground for the New Headquarters Building.**

Right **Vice President George W. Bush, former DCI, joins President Reagan and DCI William J. Casey in breaking ground for the New Headquarters Building. As vice president, George Bush laid the Cornerstone for the NHB on November 1, 1985. Employees began moving into the building in June 1988.**

Contents for Posterity

Vice President George W. Bush presided at the laying of the Cornerstone and dedication of the New Headquarters Building on November 1, 1985. In preparation for the ceremony, Agency employees were invited to suggest documents and other materials to be sealed within the Cornerstone. Items that would provide historic perspective as well as current examples of Agency endeavors were selected. Here are the items in the Cornerstone Box, as listed in the dedication program:

1 A copy of the CIA Credo which sets forth the objectives and ideals governing our work in intelligence.

2 A CIA medallion which is representative of that given to all employees upon retirement from service.

3 The program, photo booklet, and text of President Reagan's speeches to covert and overt employees at the Groundbreaking Ceremony on May 8, 1984.

4 A copy of the current editions of the *World Fact Book*, containing political, geographic, and economic facts of all other countries in the world, and of the *Fact Book on Intelligence*.

5 The publication *Directors and Deputy Directors of CIA: Dates and Data 1946-1983*.

6 A miniature agent camera and crypto chip with a brief description of their use and technology employed.

7 An aerial photograph of the CIA Headquarters complex before construction of the new building.

8 An artist's rendering of the new building as it will appear when completed.

9 Remarks of the DCI, William J. Casey, at Westminster College in Fulton, Missouri, on October 29, 1983.

10 Remarks of the DDCI, John N. McMahon, at the memorial service for Beirut Embassy victims on April 29, 1983.

11 The program and Vice President's remarks at the Cornerstone Ceremony on November 1, 1985.

Right **Vice President George W. Bush (left) and DCI William J. Casey flank President Ronald W. Reagan after the ground-breaking ceremony for the New Headquarters Building on May 8, 1984. Two years earlier, on June 23, 1982, President Ronald W. Reagan visited the CIA to sign into law the Intelligence Identities Protection Act of 1982, Public Law 97-200. The law imposes criminal penalties on those who reveal the names of covert intelligence persons.**

Left Employees require parking space. This is the parking deck built downhill to the west of the New Headquarters Building. It added capacity for hundreds of vehicles. The site for the NHB is above the parking deck. Note the two clusters of trees saved between the NHB site and the parking deck.

Opposite page **With the completion of the New Headquarters Building and parking structure, the Langley complex evolved into its present form. This view is to the west.**

Back when the CIA was planning to move from downtown to Langley, Allen Dulles set forth the guiding principles for creation of the headquarters compound. Those principles of creating a pastoral setting that assured privacy and security governed the expansion, just as they had guided the original establishment of the CIA headquarters on the Langley site.

Design and Construction

Smith, Hinchman & Grylls Associates, a Detroit architectural and engineering firm, was chosen to design the expansion. Among the firm's many achievements were the Dirksen Senate Office Building near the Capitol and the ARCO Tower in Dallas. The National Capital Region office of the General Services Administration was the contract agent. The George Hyman Construction Company prepared the site and constructed the foundation. The Centex Construction Company was the builder.

The New Headquarters Building was the major element in the expansion. Other elements included construction of a covered three-level parking deck and connections to the existing building and cafeteria. In addition, a new visitor center and security checkpoint were constructed along the main entrance drive to improve and expedite security procedures.

The expansion was designed to provide high-quality office space and the ancillary uses necessary to support the administrative, analytical, and operational needs of the CIA. In fact, the New Headquarters Building is considered a multipurpose facility because it consists of both office

"...We have a responsibility to assure the American people that they have the best intelligence service in the world, and that it is staffed by honorable men and women who work within the framework of our laws and our shared values."

President Ronald W. Reagan

and equipment space in its 1.1 million square feet.

President Reagan led a group of dignitaries in the groundbreaking ceremonies for the NHB on May 8, 1984. Construction moved swiftly. George Bush, then the vice president, laid the Cornerstone on November 1, 1985. The first employees began moving into the building in June 1988, and by March 1991 the expansion was completed and all occupants were in place. A few thousand employees from the Washington metropolitan area were relocated to the office spaces of the NHB.

The parking deck provides covered parking for hundreds of vehicles. It is built into a small hillside and has surface access at each level, which eliminates the need for interior ramps between levels. Its low-profile design complements the campus atmosphere and is not disruptive to the neighbors such as the Claude Moore Colonial Farm and the Turner Fairbanks highway research station.

Blending into the Site

Addition of the New Headquarters Building (NHB) preserved the campus atmosphere and wooded environment of the site. Also, under the expansion plan, the Original Headquarters Building remained the principal and ceremonial entrance into the CIA headquarters.

The expansion design is harmonious with the topography of the site, with the NHB actually set into the hillside west of the cafeteria. The building consists of two six-story office towers constructed of green-tinted glass curtain walls. Their horizontal and vertical divisions were designed to be compatible with the existing Original Headquarters

Left This view of the New Headquarters Building entrance shows the major use of glass in its design.

Building facade. The ground floor exterior base was constructed of concrete to resemble the OHB. It contains building support functions such as loading docks.

Entrance into the NHB proper is at the fourth floor level on the west side. The parking deck is downhill, about 400 feet away. The entrance is framed by an arching glass and steel structure. It is visually pleasing and inviting. The approach is flanked by greenery. About sixty percent of the Agency staff walk into the building through this entrance because it is closest to the parking deck and other parking lots on the campus.

First impressions when entering the building are of light and space. The sky is visible through arched overhead glass. The light is ever-changing according to time of day and weather and cloud conditions.

A plaque of William J. Casey is mounted on the north wall of the fourth floor lobby. Casey was DCI for six years, from January 28, 1981, to January 29, 1987. The NHB was designed and built during his tenure. His image is sculpted in Virginia slate against a background of green serpentine stone.

The construction of the interior of the NHB was designed to allow swift reconfiguration of office spaces at minimum cost. A system of plug-in wiring is used for electrical distribution. The entire office and computer spaces are on raised flooring. The air-conditioning system is flexible, easily adaptable to reconfigurations of interior space. Energy conservation has been emphasized throughout the NHB. The most noticeable evidence is the unique double wall exterior. This double wall provides an insulating barrier on all sides.

After passing down the entrance hallway and through the security checkpoint, a visitor is able to appreciate the openness of the design. Toward the east is a view of the cafeteria, with the sky visible. The view downward is of the NHB Atrium.

The four-story Atrium on the east side of the NHB contains an employee services concourse and exhibit areas. Its four levels of outdoor planters replace some of the greenery lost during construction. Two escalators expedite the movement of people between the fourth and first floors.

The NHB Atrium may be likened to a village square. It is situated at the confluence of pedestrian routes between the original and new buildings, and to and from the cafeteria. It is an appropriate place for displaying exhibits on themes of interest to Agency employees. The Fine Arts Commission manages the periodic exhibits here and similar exhibits displayed on the first floor of the Original Headquarters Building.

The CIA's Work and Family Center is located in the Atrium. The center is evidence of the Agency's commitment to addressing employee concerns on important matters. It is an umbrella organization that combines the services of offices and programs that focus on personal and family issues.

"Intelligence is and always will be our first line of defense, enabling us to ward off emerging threats whenever possible before any damage is done. It can also be a means of anticipating opportunities."

President George W. Bush

In the Center, knowledgeable employees and a variety of resources are available to assist employees with making informed life decisions. Staff members provide information, make referrals for service, and answer questions about work concerns or family situations that are important to employees.

Employees may make use of a variety of services at the Center. They include a personnel services counter, career center, house hunters, resource area, seminars, casualty assistance, family and employee liaison office, medical leave bank, and exit processing.

Presidential Visits

During President Ronald W. Reagan's first term, the United States responded to the 1979 Soviet invasion of Afghanistan by beginning to aid the Afghan mujahidin. President Reagan also directed the CIA to support the anti-Communist Contras who were fighting against the Sandinista regime in Nicaragua. By the end of his second term, the Soviet Union had abandoned its adventure in Afghanistan, and in Europe, the Communist empire was beginning to crumble.

William J. Casey, who led the CIA during this era, died on January 29, 1987. The Deputy DCI, Robert M. Gates, served as acting Director until Casey's successor was confirmed. William H. Webster became Director of Central Intelligence on May 26, 1987. At Webster's swearing-in ceremony, President Reagan spoke about the continued need for first-class intelligence:

Left **Plaque at the right side of the entrance to NHB, at the fourth-floor level. This entrance is used by the majority of employees.**

"...We have a responsibility to assure the American people that they have the best intelligence service in the world, and that it is staffed by honorable men and women who work within the framework of our laws and our shared values.

"[But] our liberty, our way of life, requires eternal vigilance. The United States cannot survive in the modern world without a vigorous intelligence agency, capable of acting swiftly and in secret."

George W. Bush became president of the United States on January 20, 1989. He is the only former Director of Central Intelligence to be elected president. The Berlin Wall was torn down during his first year in office, and the Soviet Union fractured soon after. The demise of the Soviet Union changed the order of things. The obvious threat of nuclear war had diminished, but other threats kept the world a dangerous place. The Iraqi invasion of Kuwait in August 1990 required a military response. American intelligence enabled President Bush to fashion a coalition of nations allied with a common purpose. American fighting men and women went to war as part of the coalition to eject Saddam Hussein's forces early in 1991.

On October 23 of that year, President Bush spoke to former members of the OSS gathered at the CIA headquarters. He paid tribute to their service in the past and then looked ahead. He said:

"[T]he challenge of the excellent men and women in Langley and elsewhere in the intelligence community, is to move beyond the Cold War to the complex problems of the

Opposite page **Looking down from the fourth floor into the Atrium of the New Headquarters Building. Scale models of U-2 (left) and SR-71 reconnaissance airplanes were donated by Lockheed Martin. The U-2 model was used in wind tunnel testing during its development for the CIA. Both aircraft types were created in the famed Lockheed "Skunk Works." Actual versions of both will be displayed at the planned expansion of the National Air and Space Museum at Dulles International Airport, scheduled to open in December 2003.**

21st century. Tomorrow's intelligence community will need to consolidate and extend freedom's gains against totalitarianism. Intelligence will enhance our protection against terrorism, against the drug menace. Intelligence will help our policymakers understand emerging economic opportunities and challenges. It will help us thwart anyone who tries to steal our technology or otherwise refuses to play by the competitive rules. It will help us seek peace and avert conflicts in regions of dangerous tension."

Three weeks later, on November 12, President Bush swore in Robert M. Gates as DCI. President Bush summarized the role of intelligence for the nation when he said:

"Intelligence is and always will be our first line of defense, enabling us to ward off emerging threats whenever possible before any damage is done. It can also be a means of anticipating opportunities."

William J. Clinton became president on January 20, 1993. He selected R. James Woolsey to succeed Robert Gates as DCI. Woolsey served in the post from February 5, 1993, until January 10, 1995. John M. Deutch followed Woolsey, taking office on May 10, 1995, and serving until December 15, 1996.

President Clinton recognized the perils of an uncertain world. With the aid of timely intelligence he sent American forces into Haiti to preserve order and to Bosnia as peacekeepers. Visiting the CIA on January 4, 1994, he highlighted the challenges for the intelligence community:

"The end of the Cold War increases our security in many ways. You helped to win that Cold War, and it is fitting that a piece of the Berlin Wall stands here on these grounds.

Left **Another perspective in the Atrium of the New Headquarters Building. No matter the season or time of day (or night), the Atrium is a refreshing passage.**

But even now, this new world remains dangerous and, in many ways, more complex and more difficult to fathom. We need to understand more than we do about the challenges of ethnic conflict, militant nationalism, terrorism, and the proliferation of all kinds of weapons. Accurate, reliable intelligence is the key to understanding each of these challenges. And without it, it is difficult to make good decisions in a crisis or in the long-term."

By the time he visited the CIA again on July 14, 1995, President Clinton had been the prime customer of the intelligence community for two and one-half years. He said during his visit:

"The intelligence I receive [every morning] informs just about every foreign policy decision we make. It's easy to take it for granted, but we couldn't do without it. Unique intelligence makes it less likely that our forces will be sent into battle, less likely that American lives will have to be put at risk. It gives us a chance to prevent crises instead of forcing us to manage them."

George J. Tenet was the Deputy DCI under John Deutch from July 3, 1995, until December 15, 1996. He became acting DCI when Deutch left. President Clinton nominated Tenet for the Directorship and he became the sixteenth Director of Central Intelligence since its founding. ●

Opposite page **President George W. Bush is flanked by DCI William H. Webster (right) and Deputy DCI Richard J. Kerr during a visit to the New Headquarters Building. Judge Webster served as DCI from May 26, 1987, to August 31, 1991. Mr. Kerr was Deputy DCI, March 20, 1989, to August 31, 1991, and acting DCI from that day until November 5, 1991.**

Right **The Work and Family Center is a focal point for employees. Its staff provide information, make referrals for service, and answer questions about work concerns or family situations important to employees.**

Left **President George W. Bush and DCI Robert M. Gates after the latter took the oath on November 6, 1991. Gates served as DCI through January 19, 1993.**

Right **R. James Woolsey, Director of Central Intelligence (center), greets Louis J. Freeh, FBI Director, at the entrance to the OHB.**

Opposite page **Lowering the American flag for the last time at the South Building on the 2430 E Street Complex. The date is July 30, 1994. DCI R. James Woolsey presided. The original sign was removed from display in the library and returned to E Street for this ceremony.**

"We need to understand more than we do about the challenges of ethnic conflict, militant nationalism, terrorism, and the proliferation of all kinds of weapons. Accurate, reliable intelligence is the key to understanding each of these challenges. And without it, it is difficult to make good decisions in a crisis or in the long-term."

President William J. Clinton

Right **DCI John M. Deutch addresses Agency employees. His tenure as DCI ran from May 10, 1995, to December 15, 1996.**

Opposite page **President William J. Clinton (right) nominated George J. Tenet to succeed John M. Deutch. Mr. Tenet, the Deputy Director from July 3, 1995, served as Acting DCI from December 1996 until July 11, 1997, when he was sworn in as Director of Central Intelligence.**

Chapter Six

Campus Tour

The campus-like atmosphere of the CIA headquarters complex is pleasing to the eye at any season of the year. It is enhanced by the harmony that exists between the man-made structures and the majority of the site that remains undeveloped. The wooded environment establishes the campus as a special place, an island of tranquillity.

Opposite page **Tour of the CIA Langley campus begins with the American flag flying in front of the Original Headquarters Building on a brilliant winter day.**

Left **The linear concrete structure of the Original Headquarters Building contrasts with the buds on trees at its entrance.**

Right **An autumn vista of the steps leading upward from the Printing and Photography Building to the entrance to the New Headquarters Building.**

Entrances and Orientation

The control points at the entrances from the George Washington Parkway and Virginia Route 123 perform necessary security control functions. However, they are minimal man-made cleared gaps within the forested perimeter of the 258-acre site. Vehicles passing through the entrances traverse the curves of the tree-lined loop road and side roads to arrive at parking areas.

From parking areas, pedestrian approaches to the buildings continue the affiliation with nature and ease the transition from travel into work space. During the walk to any entrance, employees and visitors are always surrounded by plants and trees. Less than ten percent of the total tree cover was removed during the expansion of the 1980s when the New Headquarters Building and parking deck were constructed. Tree plantations were created after construction was done. Trees were also planted on slopes bordering the parking deck and near the NHB's west side. Total tree cover has increased as those plantings have survived and begun to mature.

The basic orientation of buildings on the site can be seen from any perspective on the walk towards the buildings. The two main buildings are on an east-west axis which extends across the site and connects to the parking deck and central utilities plant. The Printing and Photography Building is at the base of the slope west of the New Headquarters Building.

The main OHB entrance distinguishes the eastern end of the axis. The approach to this entrance is pleasant and

During the walk to any entrance, employees and visitors are always surrounded by plants and trees. Less than ten percent of the total tree cover was removed during the expansion of the 1980s when the New Headquarters Building and parking deck were constructed.

Opposite page **The Headquarters Auditorium's elegant hemispheric design complements the trees at the beginning of springtime.**

well-scaled and creates a feeling of ceremonial importance. The memorial walls on left and right inside the doors in the OHB reinforce that ceremonial feeling. Almost all visitors enter here, but only about ten percent of Agency employees do so. Another thirty percent of the employees enter the OHB through other entrances on the ground and first floors of the building.

The buildings extend westward along the axis past the cafeteria and to the fourth floor entrance into the NHB. About sixty percent of persons going into and out of the headquarters use this entrance. The elevation of the fourth floor entrance to the NHB is fifty feet higher than the main entrance to the OHB.

Architects looking at the site and its patterns of entry have drawn an analogy between the headquarters building complex and a center-hall colonial house with a detached garage in the back. In that style, the garage provides the parking and is most often used for entry into the house. The grand front entrance facing the street is used very little. That analogy may be apt, but it ignores the ever-present interaction between the man-made structures of the buildings and the infinite variety of nature seen throughout the grounds. The courtyards exemplify the relationship.

Courtyards were part of the original design. They were included in design for the expansion when the NHB and parking deck were built. The additional courtyard space between the original and new buildings preserves the large trees near the cafeteria. Additional plantings, park benches, tables, and pathways are provided to encourage use of this

Right Capt. Nathan Hale was the first American spy to die in service to his country. This statue was designed by sculptor Bela L. Pratt. British authorities on Long Island executed Hale by hanging on September 22, 1776. His last words were, "I regret that I have but one life to lose for my country."

Left **Sculptor Bela L. Pratt depicted Nathan Hale on the gallows, hands bound, before his execution. The original was erected at Yale in 1914. This replica was erected at the CIA in 1973, 200 years after his graduation from Yale. It is situated between the Original Headquarters Building and the Headquarters Auditorium. Hale was born on June 6, 1755, in Coventry, Connecticut.**

space by Agency employees. From the cafeteria and from the Atrium of the NHB this major courtyard creates a pleasant view during any time or season, and under any weather conditions.

Art on the Campus Grounds

Besides the natural foliage and the landscaping of the grounds, several pieces of art enhance the appearance of the campus. They fall within the purview of the Fine Arts Commission.

The life-size statue of Nathan Hale on the right side of the OHB entrance provides human scale contrasting with the dominance of the seven-story structure. Hale's figure with his hands bound is a reminder of the importance of intelligence in the struggle for American independence. Nathan Hale may be called the nation's first intelligence agent. He was a captain in Gen. George Washington's army who volunteered for an espionage mission on Long Island to gain information on the British occupation forces. Hale posed as a schoolteacher, wearing a brown civilian suit instead of his army uniform. The British captured him, tried him as a spy, and executed him by hanging on September 22, 1776. He was twenty-one.

Hale's statue was the first work of art to be placed outside on the headquarters grounds. It was erected in 1973 on the bicentennial of Hale's graduation from Yale University. According to Yale University, this statue is the second replica of the original designed by Bela L. Pratt, himself an 1898 Yale graduate. Its history is told in the Summer 1988 issue of *Yale Alumni* magazine, in an article

Right **This slab sunk into the ground at the NHB entrance begins the sculpture *Kryptos* by Washington, DC, artist James Sanborn. It is one of two slabs that employees pass between to enter the building. They are red granite to recall the natural stone outcroppings, into which a layer of copper has been inserted. One is inscribed with a message in simple Morse code. The other contains a compass rose and piece of lodestone.**

by Judith Ann Schiff titled, "Old Yale: Nathan Hale's Many Faces." The statue was erected on the campus in 1914. The first replica was erected in 1923 at Hale's birthplace in Coventry, Connecticut. It was moved to the Department of Justice in Washington in 1948.

The Fine Arts Commission of the CIA is concerned with meeting high esthetic standards outside the buildings as well as inside. The landscaping and artwork on the grounds enhance and reinforce those inside.

When the New Headquarters Building was almost ready for occupancy, a "Statement of Principles for Art for the New Building" was written. It said:

"People are the principal resource of the Central Intelligence Agency. It is their intellectual and physical energies that ultimately provide the national policymakers with superior information and analyses—the basis to formulate policies necessary to maintain this country's position in the world. An esthetically pleasing work environment at its Headquarters is an important stimulus to the efforts of those officers assigned here."

The principles were used in guiding artists competing for a $250,000 commission to create original art for the New Headquarters Building. The acquisition was part of the Art-in-Architecture program for Federal Buildings, overseen by the General Services Administration (GSA).

The CIA specified clear design criteria for the competition. The design proportions were to be "on a scale and scope commensurate with the environment, and be visually engaging to the pedestrian. It should be forceful in style

Left **James Sanborn's sculpture *Kryptos* for the Central Intelligence Agency is a three-part installation which begins outside the entrance to the New Headquarters Building with the red granite slabs. This photo shows the major element of *Kryptos*. It graces the northwest corner of the courtyard on the patio to the NHB. The curves of the large S-shaped copper screen suggest paper coming out from a computer printer. The copper is cut with a special message using 2,000 letters of the alphabet and encoded using frequency tables. The sculpture was dedicated on November 3, 1990. At the ceremony, Sanborn gave DCI William Webster a triple-sealed envelope containing the solution to the message.**

Right **The copper screen of *Kryptos* is supported on one side by a petrified tree representing the source of paper, with a whirlpool at its base, suggesting the destination of information which disappears. Jim Sanborn was born in Washington, DC, in 1945. He attended the Art and Archeology Program at Oxford University in Great Britain and received a Bachelor of Arts from Randolph-Macon College in Ashland, VA, and a Master of Fine Arts from Pratt Institute in New York, NY. He lives and works in Washington, DC.**

and manner; and be breathtaking in its beauty." The design criteria also noted the cosmopolitan nature of the Agency staff and visitors, and stipulated that the new art "must be equally worldly, yet have identifiable American roots, either in concept, materials, or representation."

A panel of six judges under chairmanship of the National Endowment for the Arts evaluated the concepts submitted for the competition. Architect William Medling was one of the judges.

The judges selected James Sanborn, a Washington artist, for the project. The Fine Arts Commission reviewed his proposal, and it was approved by the DCI in November 1988.

Sanborn's sculpture, *Kryptos*, met the principles and criteria. It begins at the entrance to the NHB where red granite and copperplate constructions are sunk into the ground on both sides of the walkway. One is a lodestone with a compass rose inscribed on it, referring to navigation. Two other parts of the sculpture are in the northwest corner of the courtyard between the NHB and the cafeteria. A petrified tree rises from a paved surface and supports a curved vertical copper plate. A small pool is partly surrounded by the copper plate. Its water is turbulent. A placid pool is located among trees in the courtyard between two massive stone outcroppings. In Sanborn's words, its water is "calm, reflective, contemplative." He told Agency employees during the construction of *Kryptos* in 1989-90 that other materials around the site, such as large stones, ornamental grasses, and small trees, were designed "to make the natural features surrounding the Agency more visually interesting and thought-provoking."

Right **Duck family of the intelligence community is well-camouflaged in the foliage in the center courtyard of the Original Headquarters Building. Agency employees enjoyed watching the ducks as they grew.**

DCI William H. Webster presided at the dedication of *Kryptos* on November 3, 1990.

The Berlin Wall went up rapidly, beginning on the night of August 13, 1961. That was about the time the first group of Agency employees prepared to move from downtown Washington into the Original Headquarters Building. Nearly three decades later, the Berlin Wall crumbled and fell. Its literal destruction foretold the collapse of Soviet-style Communism that happened in the following two years. Mikhail Gorbachev's resignation at Christmas of

Right **The Berlin Wall came down in November 1989, a precursor to the collapse of Communism. A memorial incorporating a section of the Wall was dedicated on December 18, 1992.**

Opposite page **Berlin Wall section is illuminated at night. Original Headquarters Building is in the background.**

Right **A pond in the courtyard brings natural beauty to the working environment.**

1991 marked the end of the Soviet Union.

The men and women of the Central Intelligence Agency contributed mightily to the collapse of the Berlin Wall and of the Soviet Union. The Fine Arts Commission felt that it was fitting that a section of the Wall should be placed on the CIA campus. It is situated along the path leading from the South parking lot to the Southwest entrance to the Original Headquarters Building. The Berlin Wall section was dedicated on December 18, 1992, during the tenure of Robert M. Gates as DCI. Another portion of the Berlin Wall is displayed in the CIA Exhibit Center in the New Headquarters Building.

The woodland setting of the CIA campus is home to the full range of bird and animal life indigenous to northern Virginia. They range from field mice to small herds of deer, and from chickadees to chicken hawks.

The wildlife may be encountered almost anywhere on the campus, but especially on the jogging trail. The path is laid out in a winding course of more than 1.2 miles through the woods and around a meadow near the south-eastern corner of the complex. Younger evergreen stands of pine and cedar have been planted in the meadow of the jogging trail, adding to the natural beauty of the trail as a place to refresh both mind and body.

This completes the tour of the CIA campus and its buildings and grounds. ●

"People are the principal resource of the Central Intelligence Agency. It is their intellectual and physical energies that ultimately provide the national policymakers with superior information and analyses—the basis to formulate policies necessary to maintain this country's position in the world. An esthetically pleasing work environment at its Headquarters is an important stimulus to the efforts of those officers assigned here."

CIA Fine Arts Commission

Right **Closer to the buildings, these picnic tables and trees create pleasant spots for eating or relaxing.**

Left **The seasons change, but the grace of the buildings' design is constant, as in this autumn scene.**

Opposite page **Springtime brings blossoms to frame the precast concrete of the Original Headquarters Building facade.**

Left **Views of the courtyard show the success of the design in creating a pastoral, campus-like setting according to the guiding principles for the Langley headquarters.**

Opposite page **Arches of the cafeteria grace the inner campus.**

This page, left **Physical fitness enhances mental alertness. A trail on campus invites joggers and walkers at all times of the year. They encounter deer, birds, and sometimes snakes.**

This page, right **Unafraid of approaching joggers, this squirrel stands its ground. It is apparently accustomed to their presence in its domain.**

Right **The caltrop is an ancient and ingenious device for obstructing enemies. One point is always directed upwards. This large example is used to block armored and other vehicles. Smaller versions are useful in impeding foot traffic.**

Left A snowblower of the Facilities Management Group clears a path from the garage for the buses to begin their daily rounds. The Facilities Management Group is responsible for maintaining the Headquarters buildings and grounds.

Right **Springtime on the
CIA campus.**

Left **A hawk poised in a tree is representative of the range of wildlife that thrives on the CIA campus.**

Right **This dove built its nest atop the dashboard of one of the Agency's motor pool buses. The bus was kept out of service until the eggs were hatched.**

Left **Solar-powered lawnmowers are quieter than their gasoline engine counterparts and do not require refueling. These two are trimming the courtyard grass.**

Right **An elite corps of handlers with trained dogs enhances security of the campus.**

Left **The changing seasons are reflected in the windows of the two headquarters buildings.**

Chapter Seven

Memorials and Tribute to the People of the CIA

*This tour of the Central Intelligence Agency headquarters at Langley concludes with
an appreciation of the memorials to Agency employees.*

IN HONOR OF THOSE MEMBERS
OF THE CENTRAL INTELLIGENCE AGENCY
WHO GAVE THEIR LIVES IN THE SERVICE OF THEIR COUNTRY

★ ★ ★ ★ ★ ★ ★ ★ ★ ★ ★ ★ ★ ★ ★ ★ ★ ★
★ ★ ★ ★ ★ ★ ★ ★ ★ ★ ★ ★ ★ ★ ★ ★ ★ ★ ★
★ ★ ★ ★ ★ ★ ★ ★ ★ ★ ★ ★ ★ ★ ★ ★ ★
★ ★ ★ ★ ★ ★ ★ ★ ★ ★ ★ ★ ★ ★ ★ ★ ★
★

It is the nature of organizations and nations to honor heroes and persons of high achievement. The lives and actions of men and women in both categories can inspire and instruct. On the national scale, George Washington and Robert E. Lee are enduring examples of American military heroes. Similarly, Thomas Edison and Alexander Graham Bell are inventors of high achievement. They are publicly lauded and their achievements serve as examples for others to emulate.

Recognizing Valor and Achievement

In the realm of American intelligence services, heroes and high achievers cannot be revealed publicly. Their exploits must remain within the shadows. They might be known to a few colleagues and family, but they are otherwise anonymous. This is the nature of intelligence service. In the case of the Central Intelligence Agency, it is also a legal requirement.

In 1949 Congress passed the Central Intelligence Agency Act as a supplement to the 1947 National Security Act. Among its provisions, it enabled the CIA to use confidential procedures for fiscal and administrative actions. The Agency could legally conceal its budget according to the 1949 Act. The CIA was also exempted from disclosing names of its personnel, their titles, and their salaries. This prevented the consequences of disclosure of intelligence sources and methods.

The provision preventing disclosure of Agency people was strengthened in 1982. President Ronald W. Reagan signed the Intelligence Identities Protection Act of

Left **Vice President Al Gore (center), DCI John M. Deutch (right), and Deputy DCI George J. Tenet step away from the Memorial Wall after placing a wreath in honor of those memorialized. Each year near Memorial Day the DCI lays a wreath in front of the Wall. Families of the fallen heroes are invited to attend the solemn occasion.**

IN HONOR OF THOSE MEMBERS
OF THE CENTRAL INTELLIGENCE AGENCY
WHO GAVE THEIR LIVES IN THE SERVICE OF THEIR COUNTRY

Around the fall of 1993 the Fine Arts Commission responded to suggestions from Agency employees to create some means, in addition to the Memorial Wall, of honoring those of the CIA who died serving the country. They also wished to recognize those who contributed to preserving the nation's security, but whose death was not job-related. After study and evaluation, the outcome was to create a Memorial Garden. Besides enhancing the campus setting, it was also conceived as a place where Agency employees could spend quiet time in contemplation or meditation and reflection in remembrance of those who have gone.

The site chosen for the Memorial Garden was a space between the Original Headquarters Building and the Headquarters Auditorium not far from the statue of Nathan Hale.

Design and construction were performed by Oehme, Van Sweden & Associates of Washington, DC, an internationally known landscape architectural firm. Funds for construction were provided via the Federal Art-in-Architecture program. Agency employees made voluntary contributions for plants and landscaping.

Construction began in the fall of 1995. The Memorial Garden was dedicated on June 7, 1996. DCI John M. Deutch delivered commemorative remarks and former DCI Richard M. Helms gave the keynote address.

Memorial services are held annually near Memorial Day.

Left **Fall 1995. The Memorial Garden site has been prepared. Original Headquarters Building is on the right and Headquarters Auditorium on the left.**

Right **Pond at the Memorial Garden is ready to receive water, aquatic plants, and fish when warm weather arrives in the spring of 1996.**

Opposite page **View of the Memorial Garden seen from upper floor of the Original Headquarters Building in spring 1996.**

Right **Serenity of the Memorial Garden, May 30, 1996. Plants in the water and on the hillside are robust, as are the fish in the pond. This was the scene a week before the Garden was dedicated.**

Left **From any position or perspective, the Memorial Garden invites contemplation and reflection.**

1982 on June 23. It imposed criminal penalties for revealing the names of covert intelligence persons.

The CIA must therefore use discretion when honoring its heroes and those who have made great achievements in the intelligence arena.

President Dwight D. Eisenhower expressed his feelings about this at the dedication of the Cornerstone for the Original Headquarters Building. He said:

"By its very nature the work of this agency demands of its members the highest order of dedication, ability, trustworthiness, and selflessness—to say nothing of the finest type of courage, whenever needed. Success cannot be advertised; failure cannot be explained. In the work of intelligence, heroes are undecorated and unsung, often even among their own fraternity. Their inspiration is rooted in patriotism—their reward can be little except the conviction that they are performing a unique and indispensable service for their country, and the knowledge that America needs and appreciates their efforts. I assure you this is indeed true."

Eisenhower delivered his comments on his appreciation of American intelligence officers on November 3, 1959. Two years later, President John F. Kennedy spoke in the same vein when he visited CIA headquarters on November 28, 1961:

"It is not always easy. Your successes are unheralded—your failures are trumpeted. I sometimes have that feeling myself, but I am sure you realize how important is your work, how essential it is—and how, in the long sweep of history, how significant your efforts will be judged."

President Richard M. Nixon acknowledged the same

Left **The Original Headquarters Building is reflected in the Memorial Garden pond.**

> *"…[H]e knew that no intelligence organization can succeed without recognizing the importance of people—people with discretion, ingenuity, loyalty, and a deep sense of responsibility to protect and promote American virtues."*
>
> **Judge William H. Webster, DCI**
> *(on the dedication of General Donovan's statue)*

sentiments when he visited the CIA on March 7, 1969. He told employees: "I know, too, that…there will be no recognition of those who have served far beyond the call of duty, because by definition where the CIA is concerned your successes must never be publicized and your failures will always be publicized."

Maj. Gen. William J. Donovan is an example of the discretion needed. Considered the "father of the CIA," Donovan earned the Medal of Honor in World War I. His gallantry in combat in that war could be recognized, but his achievements in directing the OSS during World War II could not be publicized.

The CIA has created a range of medals to honor service, achievement, and valor. The two most prestigious are the Distinguished Intelligence Cross and the Distinguished Intelligence Medal.

The Distinguished Intelligence Cross is awarded "for a voluntary act or acts of extraordinary heroism involving the acceptance of existing dangers with conspicuous fortitude and exemplary courage."

The Distinguished Intelligence Medal is presented "for performance of outstanding services or for achievement of a distinctly exceptional nature in a duty or responsibility."

The public is unaware of the occasions when the Agency awards those and other medals to deserving men and women. Those receiving such medals do not expect or seek public recognition for their achievements.

Left **DCI John Deutch and former DCI Richard Helms (right) lead a moment of reflection during dedication of the new Memorial Garden site, June 7, 1996. Sen. John Glenn (D-Ohio) stands at attention in the row on left.**

The Memorial Walls

Medals are one type of recognition. Memorials are another. Arlington National Cemetery, seven miles downstream from the Agency, is a memorial which is the final resting place for more than 225,000 persons. The Iwo Jima Memorial and Vietnam War Memorial are near Arlington on opposite banks of the Potomac.

On two special walls in the foyer of the Original Headquarters Building are memorials to intelligence heroes. The OSS Memorial is on the south wall, on the left as one enters.

The legend inscribed on the wall, which matches that of the Central Intelligence Agency's Memorial Wall opposite, pays tribute to the nameless heroes:

"In honor of those members of the Office of Strategic Services who gave their lives in the service of their country."

A single star is on the wall beneath this inscription. Before the wall stands a life-size statue of General Donovan, with a Book of Honor citing the names of those who gave their lives in OSS service. Larry Ludtke sculpted the statue.

General Donovan's statue was dedicated on October 28, 1988, and the complete OSS Memorial was dedicated on June 12, 1992. At the dedication of General Donovan's statue, Judge William H. Webster, Director of Central Intelligence, said: "…[H]e knew that no intelligence organization can succeed without recognizing the importance of people—people with discretion, ingenuity, loyalty, and a deep sense of responsibility to protect and promote American virtues."

The CIA Memorial Wall is located on the north side of the foyer, on the right as one enters. The Fine Arts Commission of the Agency commissioned it in 1973. Harold Vogel sculpted it, completing the work in July 1974. The inscription reads, "In honor of those members of the Central Intelligence Agency who gave their lives in the service of their country." In mid-1997, seventy stars are carved into the marble wall, each representing one of those persons permanently immortalized here.

Below the stars, protected in a glass case, is the Book of Honor. It displays the years and names of those who can be revealed and the years that they died. For each of those who must be mourned in secret, a star appears in the book in the chronological order of their deaths.

An annual ceremony is held at the Memorial Wall near Memorial Day to commemorate Agency employees who lost their lives in the line of duty.

The Memorial Garden

Outside the Original Headquarters Building is another tribute to deceased men and women who have supported the Agency's mission. It is the Memorial Garden, a tranquil place conducive to thought. Its genesis dates back to the fall of 1993. Agency employees had suggested to the Fine Arts Commission that something should be created in remembrance of those who died in service to the country but were not immortalized on the Memorial Wall, or whose careers contributed to national security but whose death was not directly related to their jobs.

The Fine Arts Commission responded to the suggestions and studied the matter. The result was the decision to create the Memorial Garden. Besides enhancing the campus setting, the Memorial Garden is a haven where Agency employees might spend quiet time in contemplation or meditation and to reflect on the memory of the deceased. Royalties from the sale of this book benefit the Memorial Garden Fund.

The site chosen for the Memorial Garden was a space between the Original Headquarters Building and the Headquarters Auditorium, north of the statue of Nathan Hale. Oehme, Van Sweden & Associates of Washington, DC, designed and constructed the Memorial Garden.

The Federal Art-in-Architecture program funded the construction. Agency employees made contributions for plants and landscaping. Construction began in the fall of 1995, and the Memorial Garden was dedicated on June 7, 1996. DCI John M. Deutch delivered commemorative remarks at the dedication, and former DCI Richard M. Helms gave the keynote address. Memorial services are held in the Garden annually near Memorial Day.

The Memorial Garden is an appropriate place to complete the tour. It gives each of us the opportunity to pause for a moment and give thanks to those quiet and anonymous men and women of the Central Intelligence Agency.

The inscription on a plaque in the Garden reads: "In memory of those whose unheralded efforts served a grateful nation."

The CIA's unending quest for the truth keeps us free. ●

Source Notes

No books have been published specifically about the CIA headquarters complex and its buildings. However, brief references appeared in the books listed below. They were helpful in undertanding the OSS years, the beginnings of the CIA, and the move into the Langley complex:

Grose, Peter. *Gentleman Spy: The Life of Allen Dulles*. Boston: Houghton Mifflin Co., 1994.

Roosevelt, Archibald. *For Lust of Knowing*. Boston: Little Brown and Co., 1988.

Troy, Thomas F. *Donovan and the CIA. A History of the Establishment of the Central Intelligence Agency*. Washington: Central Intelligence Agency, Center for the Study of Intelligence, 1981.

Turner, Stansfield. *Secrecy and Democracy; The CIA in Transition*. Boston: Houghton Mifflin Co., 1985.

Several pamphlets and brochures produced by the CIA for public release were helpful. Among them were:

CIA Center for the Study of Intelligence. "Our First Line of Defense," Presidential Reflections on U.S. Intelligence. (January 1996).

Central Intelligence Agency. *Fact Book on Intelligence*. April 1985 and June 1995 editions.

The CIA's Web site on the Internet was another fruitful source. It may be reached at http://www.odci.gov/cia

The General Services Administration Art-in-Architecture Project Report, Item #AA215, contained much useful material about James Sanborn's sculpture *Kryptos*.

An article by Judith Ann Schiff titled "Old Yale: Nathan Hale's Many Faces," from *Yale Alumni* magazine of Summer 1988 helped with background on Hale's life and the statues of him.

Index